Student Workbook

for

Williams, Sawyer, and Wahlstrom

Marriages, Families, and Intimate Relationships
A Practical Introduction

prepared by

Kenneth L. Smylie
Santa Fe Community College

PEARSON

Boston   New York   San Francisco
Mexico City   Montreal   Toronto   London   Madrid   Munich   Paris
Hong Kong   Singapore   Tokyo   Cape Town   Sydney

ISBN 0-205-46397-5

Printed in the United States of America

10 9 8 7 6 5 4 3 2 1   10 09 08 07 06 05

Table of Contents

Preface

Welcome to your Student Workbook to accompany *Marriages, Families, & Intimate Relationships* by Brian K. Williams, Stacey C. Sawyer, and Carl M. Wahlstrom.

To assist you in your study of the text, the Student Workbook includes learning objectives, chapter summary, chapter outline, key terms with definitions, key people with definitions, 25 multiple-choice questions, answer key, and sample project suggestions. Use the Student Workbook along with your main text to maximize your learning.

I hope you enjoy using the Student Workbook as an aide to your reading of the text.

I dedicate this work to my loving family members, Marki, Scott, Nichole, and Tiffany. Thank you for your continuous understanding and patience in all my educational endeavors.

Kenneth L. Smylie, Ph.D.
Adjunct Instructor of Social and Behavioral Sciences
Santa Fe Community College
Gainesville, Florida
January, 2005

Successful Study Strategies for Students

There are certain basic behaviors that good students share in common. Top among these behaviors would be to make up your mind that excelling in school is important to you and is to be your **highest academic priority**.

A primary activity of all successful students is to **study** the material covered in class and in the text. Studying usually means finding a quiet spot where you can read, think, and mentally explore the concepts presented to you in your book and lectures by the instructor. You study by focusing your mental powers of attention on the facts, ideas, and information you feel the instructor and the text has emphasized as important with the intent of understanding and remembering.

All successful students make a serious effort to **attend every class**. You simply plan your day around being at the classes you are taking. Many instructors include attendance as part of your grade.

At the start of the semester you will be given a syllabus, which is a written outline describing the class content, expectations, and assignments. Your reading assignments and homework will be listed in the syllabus. Successful students pay attention to the class requirements and **do the homework** and **complete the reading assignments** on time.

The quality level of all assignments you turn in is a reflection of you and your attitude toward learning and toward the class you are attending. It is important to write in a way that is easy to read and understand. Papers should be clean, organized, and make clear sense. All work turned in should **be on time** as required by the syllabus.

When listening to the instructor's lectures, **learn to take notes** of key concepts and phrases. Research indicates that a full 80% of new material can be recalled if you review your notes within 24 hours. Many students find rewriting their notes in full sentences and clearer handwriting is helpful for review before exams.

All of the activities mentioned above require you as a student to develop and **exercise self-discipline**. Successful students have learned to live disciplined and orderly lives that revolve around their goal of academic accomplishment and learning.

Chapter 1 SEEKING:

Finding Happiness in Relationships in a Complex World

Learning Objectives

At the end of the chapter, you ought to be able to answer the following questions:
1. How could an intimate relationship make me happy?
2. What are the principal components of intimacy, marriage, and family?
3. What are the benefits of the family and what economic and demographic trends are affecting it?

Chapter Summary

1.1 Seeking Happiness through Love and Intimacy
- One way people seek happiness is through an intimate relationship with another person. Happiness is influenced both by one's genetic makeup and one's social environment. Happy people tend to spend the majority of their time with friends and family and relatively little time alone. Married people tend to be among the happiest of people and tend to have the highest levels of emotional well-being.
- Happy couples exhibit five key traits in their relationship: (1) good communication, (2) flexibility, (3) emotional closeness, (4) compatible personalities, and (5) agreement on how to handle conflict.

1.2 Intimacy, Marriage, and Family
- Intimacy is the experiencing of the essence of one's self in intense intellectual, physical, and/or emotional communion with another human being across the three dimensions of (1) breadth, (2) openness, and (3) depth.
- Compared to unmarried people, married people tend to get happier over time. Unrealistic expectations about marriage may prevent the achievement of happiness in a marriage.
- Heterosexual marriage can be defined as a socially approved mating relationship.
- Most people in North America marry for love, other cultures favor arranged marriages.
- Cohabitation, or living together, requires no license, but marrying does, which has legal implications that affect property, children, debts, and inheritance.

- Common-law marriage, in which a couple living together presents themselves as being married, is legally recognized in several states.
- For many people, a marriage or sexual relationship involves monogamy, with a person committed exclusively to one partner. Polygamy is when a person is married to several spouses. Polygyny is when a husband has more than one wife. Polyandry is when a wife has more than one husband.
- The main function of marriage is to provide a stable framework for bearing, nurturing, socializing, rearing, and protecting children.
- A traditional family is defined as a unit made up of two or more people who are related by blood, marriage, or adoption.
- The nuclear family consists of a father, mother, and children living in one household.
- Family structure has evolved beyond the nuclear family into new forms called the postmodern family; examples would be the binuclear family and the blended or stepfamily.
- Postmodern families may consist of kin that are defined as one's relatives by blood, marriage, or relationship, or, affiliated kin who are unrelated individuals who are treated as if they are related.

1.3   The Challenges to Relationships and Families Today
- Traditional family structure has been and continues to be influenced by both economic and demographic trends.
- Living in a family offers four benefits: (1) economic, (2) proximity, (3) familiarity, (4) continuity.
- Economic forces have compelled families to change from a philosophy of familism to individualism.
- Globalization (the trend toward a more interdependent world economic system) affects the U.S. economy and in turn affects the stability and happiness of families.

Chapter Outline

- One way people seek happiness is through an intimate relationship with another person. Happiness is influenced by both one's genetic makeup and one's social environment. Happy people tend to spend the majority of their time with friends and family and relatively little time alone. Married people tend to be among the happiest of people and tend to have the highest levels of emotional well-being.

1.1   SEEKING HAPPINESS THROUGH LOVE AND INTIMACY

Major Question: How could an intimate relationship make me happy?

a.   Marriage & Well-Being
  i.   Who says they are "very happy"?
    - 40% of those married
    - 24% of those living together
    - 22% of those who have never married
    - 18% of those previously married

b.   Love, Appreciation, & Happiness
  i.   Psychologist Dan Baker believes humans can manage emotions (grief, agony, sadness, etc.) for happiness.

How Happy Are You in a Relationship?
  ii.   Happy couples exhibit five key traits in their relationship:
    1. good communication
    2. flexibility
    3. emotional closeness
    4. compatible personalities
    5. agreement on how to handle conflict.

1.2   INTIMACY, MARRIAGE, AND FAMILY

Major Question: What are the principal components of intimacy, marriage, and family

a.   What is the Expression of Intimacy? The Three Dimensions of Breadth, Openness, & Depth
  i.   Intimacy is the experiencing of the essence of one's self in intense intellectual, physical, and/or emotional communion with another human being across the three dimensions of:
    1. Breadth: "What is the Range of Our Shared Activities?"—Considers the range of activities you and your partner share.
    2. Openness: "How Trusting Are We in Making Self-Disclosures to Each Other?"—describes the extent in which you and your partner disclose to one another.
    3. Depth: "How Deeply Do We Share Core Aspects of Ourselves?"—Occurs when two individuals share their innermost feelings.
  ii.   Is Deep Intimacy Really Attainable?
    1. Compared to unmarried people, married people tend to get happier over time. Unrealistic expectations about marriage may prevent the achievement of happiness in a marriage.

b.   What is Marriage?
  i.   Heterosexual marriage can be defined as a socially approved mating relationship.
  ii.   There are five components of marriage:
    1. The Emotional Component: Is Love Necessary?—Most people in North America marry for love, other cultures favor arranged marriages.

2. The Ceremonial Component: Church, State, or Other?—All cultures have ceremonies for establishing the union between two people.
3. The Legal Component: Does the State Have to Be Involved?—Cohabitation, or living together, requires no license, but marrying does, which has legal implications that affect property, children, debts, and inheritance. Common-law marriage, in which a couple living together presents themselves as being married, is legally recognized in several states.
4. The Sexual-Faithfulness Component: Are Monogamy & Exclusivity Required?—For many people, a marriage or sexual relationship involves monogamy, with a person committed exclusively to one partner. Polygamy is when a person is married to several spouses. Polygyny is when a husband has more than one wife. Polyandry is when a wife has more than one husband.
5. The Parenting Component: Are Children the Main Reason for Marriage?—The main function of marriage is to provide a stable framework for bearing, nurturing, socializing, rearing, and protecting children.

c. What is a Family?
  i. A traditional family is defined as a unit made up of two or more people who are related by blood, marriage, or adoption.
  ii. The Formerly "Modern" Family: The Nuclear Family -- The nuclear consists of a father, mother, and children living in one household.
  iii. Today's "Postmodern" Family: Binuclear & Blended Families -- Family structure has evolved beyond the nuclear family into new forms called the postmodern family, examples would be the binuclear family and the blended or stepfamily.
  iv. The Extended Family: Kin & Affiliated Kin -- Postmodern families may consist of kin that are defined as one's relatives by blood, marriage, or relationship, or, affiliated kin who are unrelated individuals who are treated as if they are related.
  v. Beyond the Household: Extended Families & Patterns of Residence – When members of families live nearby to each other, families begin to establish residence as neolocal, patrilocal, and matrilocal.

1.3 THE CHALLENGES TO RELATIONSHIPS AND FAMILIES TODAY
Major Question: What are the benefits of the family, and what economic and demographic trends are affecting it?
- Traditional family structure has been and continues to be influenced by both economic and demographic trends.

a. Why Have Families at All? Four Benefits
    i. Living in a family offers four benefits:
        1. Economic Benefits: Economies of Scale – families offer economic benefits due to savings in time and money.
        2. Proximity: Convenience – families provide more resources because they are in close proximity to one another.
        3. Familiarity: At Your Best & at Your Worse – family members have seen the bad and good sides of each other's personalities.
        4. Continuity: People Who are Always There for You
b. Today's Changing Families: Economic Trends
    i. The Effect of the Industrial Revolution: From Familism to Individualism – Economic forces have compelled families to change from a philosophy of familism to individualism.
    ii. Technological Change: More Complexity or More Choices?
    iii. Globalization – Globalization (the trend toward a more interdependent world economic system) affects the U.S. economy and in turn affects the stability and happiness of families.
    iv. The Mass Media & Popular Culture: Relief from Boredom & Other Effects
c. Today's Changing Families: Demographic Trends
    i. Changes in Ethnic & Racial Diversity
    ii. The Changes in the Postmodern Family
d. Your Personal Exploration

Key Terms

Affiliated kin: unrelated individuals who are treated as if they are related. p. 16
Beliefs: the definitions and explanations people have about what is true. p. 22
Binuclear family: a family in which members live in two different households. p. 15
Blended family: or stepfamily, created when two people marry and one or both brings into the household a child or children from a previous marriage or relationship. p. 15
Common-law marriage: a type of living arrangement in which a man and a woman living together present themselves as being married and are legally recognized as such. p. 13
Demographics: the study of population characteristics, such as family size, marriage and divorce rates, and ethnicity and race. p. 22
Demography: the study of population and population characteristics. p. 22
Ethnicity: the cultural characteristics that distinguish one group from another. p. 23
Extended family: family members that include the nuclear family and others as well, such as uncles and aunts, nieces and nephews, cousins, grandparents. p. 16
Familism: when decisions are made, family collective concerns take priority over individual concerns. p. 19
Family: traditionally defined as a unit of two or more people who are related by blood, marriage, or adoption and who live together. p. 14
Family of origin: the family into which you were born or in which you grew up. p. 15

Family of procreation: the family you begin if and when you get married and have children. p. 15

Globalization: the trend of the world economy toward becoming a more interdependent system. p. 21

Individualism: when decisions are made, individual concerns take priority over family collective concerns. p. 20

Intimacy: intense affection for, commitment to, and sharing of intellectual, physical, and emotional connections with another person. p. 9

Kin: relatives by blood, marriage, remarriage, or adoption, ranging from grandparents to nieces to brothers-in-law. p. 16

Marriage: a socially approved mating relationship. p. 12

Matrilocal residence: the situation in which newly married partners reside with the wife's family. p. 16

Monogamy: a marital or sexual relationship in which a person is committed exclusively to one partner. p. 13

Modern family: or nuclear family, consists of father, mother, and children living in one household. p. 15

Neolocal residence: describes the situation in which newly married partners set up their own household, not connected with the bride or groom's parents. p. 16

Nuclear family: or modern family, consists of father, mother, and children living in one household. p. 15

Patrilocal residence: describes the situation in which newly married partners live with the husband's family. p. 16

Polyandry: a marriage in which one wife has more than one husband. p. 13

Polygamy: a marriage in which one person has several spouses. p. 13

Polygyny: a marriage in which one husband has more than one wife. p. 13

Postmodern family: describes the great variability in family forms, such as single-parent families and child-free couples. p. 15

Race: describes inherited physical characteristics that distinguish one group from another. p. 23

Roles: the pattern of behaviors expected of a person who occupies a certain social position within a certain group or culture. p. 22

Stepfamily: or blended family, created when two people marry and one or both brings into the household a child or children from a previous marriage or relationship. p. 15

Traditional family: a family in which the man's role is primarily husband, father, and income earner and the woman's role is wife, mother, and homemaker. p. 15

Values: deeply held beliefs and attitudes about what is right and wrong, desirable and undesirable. p. 22

Key People

Baker, Dan: psychologist and director of the Life Enhancement Program, author of *What Happy People Know.*

Berners-Lee, Tim: created the World Wide Web in 1991.

Diener, Ed: University of Illinois psychologist, serious researcher of happiness.

Drucker, Peter: acclaimed management theorist.

Giddens, Anthony: noted sociological theorist.

Goode, William: noted family sociologist.

McLuhan, Marshall: noted communication philosopher who coined the term "global village."

Murdock, Robert: anthropologist, who in 1949 coined the term "nuclear family."

Olson, David: pioneering University of Minnesota family researcher.

Seligman, Martin: University of Pennsylvania psychologist, director of the Positive Psychology Network, author of *Authentic Happiness.*

Practice Test

1. As one 12-year study found, marriages today can be described as:
   A. conflicted
   B. irrelevant
   C. turbulent
   D. vitalized

2. Common media myths include which one of the following:
   A. civil unions are just as valid as legal marriages
   B. there is not a soul mate for each of us
   C. the main source of social problems is family breakdown
   D. love is not enough to make one happy

3. According to the scholarly evidence, the two factors that matter most in happiness are:
   A. sex and love
   B. marriage and sex
   C. religious belief and marriage
   D. money and love

4. In the text, Seligman describes three categories of levels of happiness. One of the categories is:
   A. the eventful life
   B. the meaningful life
   C. the contented life
   D. the fun-filled life

5. Psychologist Dan Baker says being happy is:
   A. the ability to practice appreciation or love
   B. taking appropriate time to rest and reflect
   C. making peace with your inner child
   D. finding a compatible soul mate

6. Pioneering family researcher David Olson found that happy couples have this relationship strength:
   A. they have opposite personalities
   B. they communicate well
   C. they are of the same race or ethnic background
   D. they are inflexible as a couple

7. According to researcher Bruce J. Biddle intimacy between you and another should be considered according to three dimensions. One of those dimensions is:
    A. openness
    B. length
    C. height
    D. sincerity

8. According to the text, marriage can be defined as
    A. a socially approved mating relationship
    B. a relationship of convenience
    C. an institution of the state
    D. a sexual, emotional, and spiritual connection

9. Polyandry is
    A. a marriage in which a husband has more than one wife
    B. a marriage in which one wife has more than one husband
    C. a marriage in which a person is committed exclusively to one partner
    D. a marriage in which one person has several spouses

10. According to the text, there are three common ways in which families establish residence. They are all of the following EXCEPT:
    A. Matrilocal
    B. Filiolocal
    C. Neolocal
    D. Patrilocal

11. The great family sociologist William Goode asserts living in a traditional family offers four benefits. One of the benefits is:
    A. community
    B. socialization
    C. continuity
    D. friendship

12. According to acclaimed management theorist Peter Drucker, every few hundred years there occurs a sharp _____ in which society rearranges itself.
    A. reevaluation
    B. transformation
    C. reformation
    D. metamorphosis

13. According to the text, today, intimacy, marriage and family life have been affected by all of the following EXCEPT:
    A. the Industrial Revolution
    B. the mass media and popular culture
    C. globalization
    D. changes in partisan politics

14. Familism is:
    A. when decisions are made, individual concerns take priority over family concerns
    B. when decisions are made, family concerns take priority over individual concerns
    C. when decisions are made, fraternal concerns take priority over sororal concerns
    D. when decisions are made, paternal concerns take priority over maternal concerns

15. The mass media and popular culture are a major source of accurate and inaccurate information affecting:
    A. our scripts
    B. our identity
    C. our values
    D. our personalities

16. Ethnicity is:
    A. the inherited physical characteristics that distinguish one group from another
    B. the cultural characteristics that distinguish one group from another
    C. the study of population and population characteristics
    D. the characteristics germane to cultural ethics

17. The largest and fastest growing minority group in the United States is:
    A. African Americans
    B. Hispanic
    C. Non-Hispanic whites
    D. Asian Americans

18. Among Non-Hispanic whites, the largest European ancestry group is:
    A. English
    B. Irish
    C. German
    D. Italian

19. According to the text, _____ are the most economically well-off racial category in the United States:
    A. Asian Americans
    B. Native Americans
    C. Hispanics
    D. African Americans

20. According to the text, since the 1800s in the United States, there have been two significant demographic trends. They are:
    A. people living longer and marrying later AND women having fewer children
    B. women having fewer children AND improved health and sanitation standards
    C. people living longer and marrying later AND improved health and sanitation standards
    D. improved health and sanitation standards AND increased geographic population movement

21. According to the text, today fewer than ____ of families can be considered nuclear or modern.
    A. 63%
    B. 25%
    C. 10%
    D. 50%

22. According to the text, changes in the Postmodern Family include:
    A. more teen marriages
    B. more non-working mothers
    C. more step families
    D. more divorces, remarriages, and blended families

23. According to the text, _____ of new marriages will eventually end in divorce at some point.
    A. 40% to 60%
    B. 30% to 50%
    C. 50% to 70%
    D. 60% to 80%

24. _____ is the trend of the world economy toward becoming a more interdependent system.
    A. Unification
    B. Globalization
    C. Solidarity
    D. Deregulation

25. According to the text, the hallmark of great civilizations has been their great systems of _____.
    A. government
    B. transportation
    C. communication
    D. education

Project Suggestions

Project 1
Ask a friend what they feel are the benefits of having or being in a family. See if their reasons are the same as those listed in the text.

Project 2
A principal theme of the text is that we seek happiness in intimate relationships. Ask three persons if they agree or disagree and why.

Project 3
Ask three faculty members what they think is the major problem facing families today and what solutions they may suggest. Write them down and reflect whether you agree or disagree.

Answer Key

1. D (p.2)	6. B (p.7)	11. C (p.17)	16. B (p.23)	21. B (p.26)
2. C (p.3)	7. A (p.10)	12. B (p.19)	17. B (p.24)	22. D (p.28)
3. C (p.5)	8. A (p.12)	13. D (p.19)	18. C (p.24)	23. A (p.28)
4. B (p.6)	9. B (p.13)	14. B (p.19)	19. A (p.25)	24. B (p.21)
5. A (p.7)	10. B (p.16)	15. C (p.22)	20. A (p.26)	25. C (p.20)

Chapter 2 UNDERSTANDING:

Learning about Intimate Behavior

Learning Objectives

At the end of the chapter, you ought to be able to answer the following questions:
1. How have the families been influenced by the past?
2. Is there a more beneficial way to approach the world and ideas than I might be taking now?
3. What are five principal kinds of scientific research?
4. What are eight perspectives for looking at the family and relationships?

Chapter Summary

2.1   A Short History of Marriage
- Family in America can be viewed from the perspective of (1) the early American era, (2) the 19th and early 20th centuries, and (3) the modern era.
- The early American family can be considered according to four groups: (1) Native American families, (2) white colonial families, (3) African American families, and (4) Hispanic (Latino) families.
- Native American families included both family structures: matrilineal (children traced their descent through their mother's line) and patrilineal (descent traced through the father's line).
- White colonial families, who were primarily of British, French, Spanish, and Portuguese origin, adhered to a Christian-influenced family model that emphasized sexual restraint, a patriarchal structure in which the father held power, and mate selection by parental arrangement rather than by love.
- The first African families to appear in North America were not slaves but indentured servants who, after fulfilling their years of service, could own land, marry, and hire out their labor. By the mid-17th century, however, the majority of black immigrants were slaves brought primarily from West Africa.
- Although Hispanic (Latino) families appeared in North America even before the New England Pilgrims, they lost most of their land through confiscation and fraud and became laborers exploited in the economic development of the Southwest. The Latino family structure was strongly influenced by familism.
- Families in the 19th and early 20th centuries were dramatically influenced by social and economic forces, including industrialization, urbanization, and immigration.

- As more people began working outside the home, the view of the family as a work unit began to decline, women felt more free to choose marriage partners for compatibility and affection, and children became less important as economic contributors.
- In the 20th century, many economic, educational, and social welfare functions began to be provided by outside agencies instead of families, and family members became more attentive to taking care of each other's emotional needs.
- The 1950s marked a return to traditional family values, as a booming economy impelled families to seek the good life in the suburbs and a stable household with a working father and stay-at-home mother.

2.2   Learning How to Think: Keys to Being Open-Minded
- Our socialization and individual life experiences result in a mind-set that affects our perceptions.
- Open-mindedness requires the development of critical thinking skills. Critical thinking means clear thinking, skeptical thinking, and active thinking.
- The best way to break through the closed habits of thought or mind-sets is to use reasoning, which involves the use of arguments.
- Mindful thinking is characterized by the creation of new categories, being open to new information, and awareness of the existence of more than one perspective.

2.3   How Do You Know What's True? Learning to Evaluate Research Results
- The five principal types of scientific research are (1) survey, (2) clinical, (3) observational, (4) experimental, and (5) cross-cultural, historical, longitudinal, and content analysis.
- Survey research uses questionnaires or interviews to collect data from small representative groups (samples).
- Clinical research entails in-depth study of individuals or small groups who have sought counseling for psychological or relationship problems from mental health professionals.
- In observational research, researchers collect data by observing people in their natural surroundings.
- In an experiment, factors or behaviors are measured or monitored under closely controlled circumstances.
- Additional research methods include cross-cultural studies, historical studies, longitudinal studies, and content analysis.

2.4   Theoretical Perspectives on the Family
- Theories are perspectives that explain why processes and events occur.
- The ecological perspective examines how a family (or individual) is influenced by and influences its environment. The structural-functional perspective views the family as a social institution that performs essential functions for society to ensure its stability.
- Conflict theory views individuals and groups as being basically in conflict with each other for power and scarce resources. The feminist perspective views the

inequality in women's roles as the result of male dominance in the family and in society.

- The symbolic-interaction perspective focuses on internal family interaction and the ongoing action and response of family members to each other. The social exchange perspective proposes that people's interactions represent the efforts of each person to maximize his or her benefits and minimize his or her costs.
- The family development perspective proposes that family members accomplish developmental tasks as they move through stages in the family life cycle. The family systems perspective suggests that family members make up a system of interconnected parts of a whole and that changes in one part change the other parts.

Chapter Outline

- The purpose of this chapter is to discuss ways to be free to think for yourself. As a way of beginning, we present a history of the American family to show how it differed from, yet led to, today's modern family.

2.1   A SHORT HISTORY OF MARRIAGE
Major Question: How have the families of today been influenced by the past?
  a. American Families in the Colonial Era
    i. Native American Families
        1. Marriage and sex: most married at young ages (between 12 and 20), most marriages were monogamous and for a lifetime, but divorce was allowed.
        2. Families: most families were small due to high infant mortality. Children were treated kindly with physical discipline uncommon.
        3. Transitions: during puberty ceremonies and rites of passage were observed.
    ii. White Colonial Families
        1. Marriage and sex: mates were usually selected by the parents and love was expected to come after marriage.
        2. Families: the family was considered an economic unit for producing goods and a social unit for taking care of family members.
        3. Transitions: children were seen as small adults and the notion of adolescence did not exist.
    iii. African American Families
        1. Marriage and sex: as slaves, blacks were prohibited from legally marrying but they legitimized their unions by their own rituals. The black culture discouraged casual sexual relationships.
        2. Families: slave families were actually far stronger than once believed and were primarily responsible for the slave's ability to survive on the plantation.
    iv. Hispanic (Latino) Families
        1. Marriage and sex: much of family life was influenced by Catholic religious teachings including rites of passage. Women were expected to

remain virgins until married but men could engage in premarital and extramarital adventures.

      2. Families: the families were seen as more important than the individual members, with the father holding all the authority and the women expected to be mothers and homemakers.

b. Families in the 19th & Early 20th Centuries
    i. Industrialization, Urbanization, & Immigration
      1. Industrialization: created changes from self-sufficient to wage-earning families and production of goods shifted from home-based human labor to machines and factories.
      2. Urbanization: as families moved to the cities and factories men became identified as the principal providers, with less contact with their extended families.
      3. Immigration: in the two waves of newcomers the "old" immigrants came mostly from western and northern Europe plus many Chinese came to the West Coast. The "new" immigrants came mostly from eastern and southern Europe, in addition, many Japanese came to the West Coast.

c. Families in the Modern Era
    i. Rise of a New Form: The Companionate Family
      1. In the 1900s, sexual attraction and compatibility began to become the basis for middle-class marriage and family relationships.
    ii. The Effect of the World Wars & the Great Depression
      1. The Great Depression—out of work men blame themselves instead of the countrywide economic condition for not being able breadwinners.
      2. World Wars I and II—women take "male-only" jobs and after the war found it difficult to leave the greater wages and freedoms of male jobs.
    iii. Families in the 1950s
      1. The Baby Boom—the swelling population, between 1946 and 1964, now makes up a third of the U.S. population.
      2. Suburbanization—the move to the suburbs from the cities allowed families to realize dreams of home ownership.
      3. The child-centered culture—influenced by Dr. Benjamin Spock mothers tended to use communication rather than physical discipline with their children.
    iv. The Family in the 1960s–2000s: In Decline?
      1. The American family is in decline, according to David Popenoe, and the family has lost its power and authority.
      2. The American family still matters, assert some sociologists, and say the high rates of divorce, fatherlessness, and working mothers had little to no negative effect.
    v. Recent History: Late 20th-Century Immigration
      1. Hispanics are the largest group of recent immigrants coming primarily from Mexico.
      2. Asians are the second largest group of recent immigrants coming from China, Philippines, and India.

2.2 LEARNING HOW TO THINK: KEYS TO BEING OPEN MINDED

Major Question: Is there a more beneficial way to approach the world and ideas than I might be taking now?

a. The Problem of Uncritical Thinking—to mix our data input with childish notions is to cripple our perception of the world around us.
   i. The Enemy: Our Mind-Sets—we see and hear what we subconsciously want to and pay little attention to facts or observations.
   ii. Critical Thinking—clear thinking involves actively seeking to understand, analyze, and evaluate information in order to solve specific problems.
b. The Steps in Critical Thinking
   i. Get an Understanding of the Problem
   ii. Gather Information & Interpret it
   iii. Develop a Solution Plan & Carry it Out
   iv. Evaluate the Plan's Effectiveness
c. Mindfulness: Take Active Control
   i. Entrapment in Old Categories versus Creation of New Ones
   ii. Automatic Behavior versus Openness to New Information
   iii. Single Perspective versus Several Perspectives
d. How to Encourage Mindfulness: Active Learning

2.3 HOW DO YOU KNOW WHAT'S TRUE? LEARNING TO EVALUATE RESARCH RESULTS

Major Question: What are five principal kinds of scientific research?

a. Survey Research: Collecting Data by Questionnaire or Interview from Representative Samples
   i. Step 1: Decide on the Population & the Sample
   ii. Step 2: Gather the Data: Using Questionnaires or Interviews
   iii. Step 3: Analyze & Generalize the Results
b. Clinical Research: In-Depth Examination of Individuals or Groups in Counseling
c. Observational Research: Observing People in Their Usual Surroundings
d. Experimental Research: Measuring Behavior under Controlled Conditions
e. Other Kinds of Research: Cross-Cultural, Historical, Longitudinal, Content Analysis
f. Trying to Be Objective: How Do You Know What's True?
i. Your Mind-Sets: The Possible Filters—personal experiences with ethnocentrism, heterosexism, and bias against not having children affect our sense of objectivity.
g. Possible Flaws in Research Studies—include researcher is biased, sample is biased, no control group, questions are not neutrally worded, time or subject distortions.

2.4 THEORETICAL PERSPECTIVES ON THE FAMILY

Major Question: What are eight perspectives for looking at the family and relationships?

a. The Ecological Perspective: The Family Is Influenced by & Influences Its Environment

b. The Structural-Functional Perspective: The Family Is a Social Institution Performing Essential Functions

c. The Conflict Perspective: Conflict & Change, Not Harmony, Is the Normal State of the Family

d. The Feminist Perspective: Inequality between Men & Women Results from Male Dominance

e. The Symbolic Interaction Perspective: People's Interactions Ultimately Determine Their Behavior

f. The Social Exchange Perspective: Individuals Seek the Most Benefits & the Least Costs in a Relationship

g. The Family Development Perspective: Individuals & Families Change through Stages of Life

h. The Family Systems Perspective: Family Members Are Interconnected, & Changes in One Affect Others

Key Terms

Adolescence: a separate social and psychological stage of development coinciding with puberty and characterized by rebellion and crises. p. 37

Appeal to authority: an argument that uses an authority in one area to pretend to validate claims in another area in which the person is not an expert. p. 51

Appeal to pity: an argument that appeals to emotion rather than arguing the merits of the case itself. p. 51

Arguments: consist of one or more premises, or reasons, logically supporting a result or outcome called a conclusion. p. 50

Case study method: clinical research that consists of clinical practitioners working directly with individuals or families using interviews, observation, and analysis of records. p. 56

Circular reasoning: an argument that rephrases the statement to be proved true. It then uses the new, similar statement as supposed proof that the original statement is in fact true. p. 50

Clinical research: entails in-depth study of individuals or small groups who have sought counseling from mental health professionals. p. 56

Companionate family: the perspective that marriage was supposed to provide romance, emotional growth, and sexual fulfillment. p. 42

Conclusion: the result or outcome of a reasoning argument. p. 50

Conflict perspective: views individuals and groups as being basically in conflict with each other for power and scarce resources. p. 64

Content analysis: the systematic examination of cultural artifacts or various forms of communication to extract thematic data and draw conclusions about social life. p. 59

Control group: subjects are not introduced to the independent variable by the researchers. p. 58

Critical thinking: means clear thinking, skeptical thinking, active thinking. p. 48

Cross-cultural studies: social scientists compare data on family life among different kinds of societies. p. 59

Deductive argument: if its premises are true, then its conclusion is true also. p. 50

Dependent variable: factors or behaviors that are affected by changes in the independent variable. p. 58

Developmental tasks: specific role expectations and responsibilities that a family member is expected to fulfill as they move through the life cycle. p. 68

Ecological perspective: examines how a family (or individual) is influenced by and influences its environment. p. 61

Ethnocentrism: the belief that one's native country, culture, language, abilities, or behaviors are superior to those of another culture. p. 60

Experiment: factors or behaviors are measured or monitored under closely controlled circumstances. p. 58

Experimental group: subjects are exposed to an independent variable introduced by the researcher. p. 58

Experimental research: researchers try to locate a single factor or behavior under controlled conditions to determine its effects. p. 58

Expressive role: according to Talcott Parsons, the female was the homemaker and was nurturing and supportive. p. 62

Fallacies: patterns of incorrect reasoning. p. 50

False cause or irrelevant reason: a type of faulty reasoning that means the conclusion does not follow logically from the supposed reasons stated earlier. p. 51

Family development perspective: proposes that family members accomplish developmental tasks as they move through stages in the family life cycle. p. 67

Family life cycle: family members' roles and relationships change, largely depending on how they have to adapt to the absence or presence of child-rearing responsibilities. p. 68

Family systems perspective: suggests that family members make up a system of interconnected parts of a whole and that changes in one part change the other parts. p. 68

Feminist perspective: the view that inequality in women's roles is the result of male dominance in the family and in society. p. 64

Generalized: whether the results of the sample can be said to apply to the population, the larger group. p. 56

Hawthorne effect: the situation in which subjects of research change from their typical behavior because they realize they are under observation. p. 57

Heterosexism: the belief that the standard family is heterosexual, with homosexual families being viewed as not true families. p. 60

Historical studies: researchers compare census, social agency, or demographic data to ascertain changing patterns of family life. p. 59

Independent variable: factors or behaviors that can be controlled or manipulated by the experimenter. p. 58

Inductive argument: if the premise is true, the conclusion is probably true, but the truth is not guaranteed. p. 50

Instrumental role: according to Talcott Parsons, the male was the breadwinner and was hardworking, self-confident, and competitive. p. 62

Interviewer bias: interviewers allow their own preconceptions to influence how they ask questions. p. 56

Irrelevant attack on opponent: an argument that attacks a person's reputation or beliefs rather than his or her argument. p. 50

Jumping to conclusions: a type of incorrect reasoning that means a conclusion has been reached when not all the facts are available. p. 50

Latent functions: are unintended, unconscious, functions with hidden purposes. p. 62

Longitudinal studies: researchers use questionnaires or interviews over a number of years to follow up on earlier investigations. p. 59

Manifest functions: are intended, open, stated, and conscious functions. p. 62

Matriarchal family: one in which the mother holds the power. p. 36

Matrilineal: children trace their descent, rights and property through the mother's line. p. 34

Mindfulness: is characterized by creation of new categories, openness to new information, and awareness of more than one perspective. p. 51

Mindlessness: is characterized by entrapment in old categories, automatic behavior, and acting from a single perspective. p. 51

Nonparticipant observation: researchers observe their subjects without interacting with them. p. 57

Nonrepresentative sample: a not scientifically valid sample where researchers pick people for convenience or availability. p. 55

Observational research: researchers obtain information data by observing people in their usual surroundings. p. 57

Participant observation: researchers interact with the subjects they are observing but do not reveal that they are researchers. p. 57

Patriarchal family: one in which the father holds the power. p. 36

Patrilineal: descent and ownership of property came down through the father's lines. p. 35

Population: describes any well-known group of people to be studied. p. 55

Premise: a point of reason used in argumentation. p. 50

Puberty: the period during which one develops secondary sex characteristics. p. 36

Questionable statistics: statistics can be misused in many ways as supporting evidence. The statistics may be unknowable, drawn from an unrepresentative sample, or otherwise suspect. p. 50

Reasoning: giving reasons in favor of an assertion and essential to critical thinking and solving life's problems. p. 50

Representative (random) sample: a sample in which everyone in your population has the same chance of being included. p. 55

Sample: describes any small group of the population to be studies. p. 55

Slippery slope: the failure to see that the first step in a possible series of steps does not lead inevitably to the rest. p. 50

Social exchange perspective: proposes that people's interactions represent the efforts of each person to maximize his or her benefits and minimize costs. p. 67

Socialization: the process by which offspring learn attitudes, beliefs, and values appropriate to their society and culture. p. 63

Stratified random sample: a sample of specific subgroups of your population in which everyone in the subgroups has an equal chance of being included in the study. p. 55

Straw man argument: an argument where one misrepresents your opponent's position to make it easier to attack, or you attack a weaker position while ignoring a stronger one. p. 50

Structural-functional perspective: views the family as a social institution that performs essential functions for society to ensure its stability. p .62

Survey research: uses questionnaires or interviews to collect data from small representative groups (samples), which are then used to generalize conclusions valid for larger groups (populations). p. 55

Symbolic interaction: refers to the process of interpersonal interaction. p. 66

Theory: a perspective or a set of statements that explains why processes and events occur. p. 61

Thomas theorem: "If people define situations as real, they are real in their consequences." p. 66

Variable: a factor that can be varied or manipulated in the experiment. p. 58

Key People

Bernard, Jessie: a feminist scholar who fueled the feminist belief that the institution of marriage oppressed women.

Blumer, Herbert: a noted proponent of the symbolic interaction perspective.

Cooley, Horton: influential sociologist during the 1920s and 1930s.

Coontz, Stephanie: author of *The Way We Never Were* and *The Way We Really Are*, writes about the American family in the 1950s.

Duvall, Evelyn: a proponent of the family development perspective and author of *Family Development*.

Langer, Ellen: the first woman to become a tenured professor of psychology at Harvard University and author of *Mindfulness* and *The Power of Mindful Living*.

Mead, George Herbert: influential sociologist during the 1920s and 1930s.

Mintz, Steven, and Kellogg, Susan: have written extensively about the history of the American family.

Parsons, Talcott: a sociologist who was the leading proponent of the structural-functional perspective in the 1950s and 1960s.

Popenoe, David: noted sociologist at Rutgers University.

Randi, James: a debunker of claims made by supporters of the paranormal.

Spock, Benjamin: author of the influential child-rearing book, *Baby and Child Care*.

Thomas, William I.: noted sociologist who developed the *Thomas theorem*.

Practice Test

1. In terms of advertising in our culture which of the following is NOT true:
   A. the average American is exposed to at least 3,000 ads every day
   B. many Americans will watch 3 years worth of TV commercials
   C. in our culture you can avoid advertising if you choose to
   D. ads make up 70% of newspapers and 40% of our mail

2. According to writer Jean Kibourne:
   A. there is a connection between advertising and our approach to marriage
   B. there is not a connection between advertising and marriage attitudes
   C. advertising has no real effect upon those who are exposed to it
   D. there is a connection between advertising and one's level of education

3. At the time of the English settlement in North America in the early 17th century there were _____ Native Americans already living there.
   A. 8 million
   B. 2 million
   C. 23 million
   D. 50 million

4. The Pueblo Indians were matrilineal, which means:
   A. they used the metric system for measurement
   B. their culture was centered around the grandparents
   C. their children traced their descent through the mother's line
   D. they used a lunar, or moon, calendar to mark time

5. In early Native American families children:
   A. were treated with great kindness and physical discipline was uncommon
   B. were sternly disciplined and punished for disobedience
   C. were seen as gifts from the Great Spirit
   D. were seen as having an evil nature needing to be purged out of them

6. The European colonists—British, French, Spanish, and Portuguese—organized their families in the _____ model.
   A. matriarchal
   B. fraternal
   C. sororal
   D. patriarchal

7.   The early Puritans allowed a visiting young male suitor to sleep in the same bed as their daughter, but the suitor would be sewn into a sack up to his neck, this practice was called:
      A.   being given the sack
      B.   bundling
      C.   bungling
      D.   none of the above, it was just a myth

8.   The notion of adolescence—a separate social and psychological stage of development coinciding with puberty and characterized by rebellion and crises:
      A.   was seen as proof that children were inherently evil
      B.   did not exist in colonial times
      C.   has been historically noted throughout the ages
      D.   is a social mythical construction

9.   As slaves, blacks were prohibited from legally marrying. Nevertheless, slaves themselves legitimized their unions by such rituals as:
      A.   exchanging rings
      B.   carving their initials in a tree
      C.   jumping over a broomstick
      D.   holding secret ceremonies

10.   The Industrial Revolution:
      A.   caused the production of goods to shift from homes to factories
      B.   was a longstanding conflict between management and labor
      C.   began in the 1950s and continues today
      D.   was a violent epoch that lasted more than a century

11.   The domination of the white European majority in the U.S. has declined from 86% in 1950 to 69% in 2000 and is projected to be _____ by 2050.
      A.   43%
      B.   28%
      C.   50%
      D.   62%

12.   Which are the largest groups of Asians immigrating to the U.S. in recent history?
      A.   Japanese, Koreans, Vietnamese
      B.   Chinese, Filipinos, Asian Indians
      C.   Native Hawaiians, Pacific Islanders, Fijians
      D.   Cambodians, Hmong, Laotians

13.   Critical thinking is best understood as _____ thinking.
      A.   active
      B.   judgmental
      C.   negative
      D.   passive

14. One type of reasoning is the "straw man argument." It means:
    A. a conclusion has been reached before all the facts are in
    B. appealing to emotion rather than arguing the merits of the case itself
    C. you misrepresent your opponent's position to make it easier to attack
    D. the first step in a possible series of steps does not lead to the rest

15. Mindfulness is best described as:
    A. passive learning
    B. active learning
    C. meditative learning
    D. single perspective learning

16. Sociologists use the term "Hawthorne effect" to refer to:
    A. observing people in their usual surroundings
    B. research based on people who have sought counseling
    C. whether the sample can be said to apply to the population
    D. subjects change their typical behavior when they know they are being observed

17. In experimental research:
    A. social scientists compare data on family life in different societies
    B. researchers try to isolate a single factor to determine its effect
    C. researchers compare demographic data to see patterns of family life
    D. researchers use interviews over a number of years to gather data

18. The ecological perspective:
    A. examines how a family is influenced by its environment
    B. views the family as a social institution performing essential functions
    C. is the process by which offspring learn beliefs in their culture
    D. views individuals as being in conflict with others for power and resources

19. The structural-functional perspective:
    A. is one of the newer perspectives in sociology
    B. explains why processes and events occur
    C. had Talcott Parsons as a leading proponent in the 1950s and 1060s
    D. considers struggle within families as natural and often desirable

20. The symbolic interaction perspective:
    A. views inequality in women's roles as the result of male dominance
    B. focuses on the ongoing action and response of family members
    C. proposes people's interactions as maximizing benefits to themselves
    D. has scholar Jessie Bernard as a noted proponent

21. A key contribution of the family development perspective:
    A. is that family members make up a system of interconnected parts
    B. is the notion of equilibrium
    C. is how members interact to make decisions and solve problems
    D. is that family members have to accomplish developmental tasks

22. The position that family members are interconnected and changes in one affect the others is part of the:
    A. family development perspective
    B. symbolic interaction perspective
    C. family systems perspective
    D. structural-functional perspective

23. The notion of equilibrium is associated with the _____ perspective.
    A. feminist
    B. conflict
    C. family systems
    D. symbolic interaction

24. The feminist perspective has been criticized:
    A. for stressing personal feelings over objectivity
    B. for stressing conflict over order
    C. for assuming people always act in rational, calculating ways
    D. for not drawing on the effects of wider social, economic, political forces

25. All of the following are aspects of the symbolic interaction perspective EXCEPT:
    A. predictability of behavior
    B. definition of the situation
    C. reduction in harassment and violence
    D. self-image based on others' interactions

Project Suggestions

Project 1
How does advertising affect you? Check out the website, *www.mediaed.org/about*, and see if you agree or disagree with what the site says about advertising.

Project 2
Talk to your parents or grandparents about family life in the 1950s and compare it to today. What has changed? What has stayed the same?

Project 3
How far can you trace your family ancestry back? Make a family tree chart. Do you notice any patterns in family names or known characteristics?

Answer Key

1. C (p.32)   6. D (p.36)   11. C (p.45)   16. D (p.57)   21. D (p.68)

2. A (p.32)   7. B (p.36)   12. B (p.46)   17. B (p.58)   22. C (p.68)

3. B (p.34)   8. B (p.37)   13. A (p.48)   18 A (p.61)   23. C (p.69)

4. C (p.34)   9. C (p.38)   14. C (p.51)   19. C (p. 62)   24. A (p.70)

5. A (p.36)   10. A (p.40)   15. B (p.53)   20. B (p.66)   25. C (p.66)

Chapter 3 GENDER:

The Meaning of Masculinity & Femininity

Learning Objectives

At the end of the chapter, you ought to be able to answer the following questions:
1. What are the principal terms anyone needs to know to discuss gender differences intelligently?
2. What are some possible explanations for gender differences?
3. Who has influenced how I feel about being a man or a woman?
4. Is there more than one way to be masculine or feminine?

Chapter Summary

3.1 Understanding Gender & Gender Roles
- Sex refers to the biological characteristics with which we were born that determine whether we are male or female. Gender refers to the socially learned attitudes and behaviors associated with being male or female.
- A gender role is the behavior expected of a female or male in a particular culture. A sex role is behavior defined by biological constraints. We learn gender roles through socialization. Gender identity is a person's psychological sense of whether he or she is male or female.
- Some people take on aspects of the roles of the other gender.
- More complicated questions of gender identity arise with transsexuals, transgenderists, and hermaphrodites.
- Most societies are patriarchal, meaning that they are male dominated, male identified, and male centered.
- Sexism is the belief that one sex is innately superior to the other. Sexual harassment is the abuse of one's position of authority to force unwanted sexual attention on someone.

3.2   Why Do Gender Roles Differ? Some Theories
- Sociobiology suggests that our social behavior—and gender behavior—results from biological differences.
- Social learning theory suggests that we learn attitudes and behaviors through our interaction with the environment.
- Blending biological and cognitive perspectives, cognitive development theory suggests that when we are children, our biological readiness in terms of our cognitive development influences how we respond to cues in the environment about gender differences.
- Some of cognitive development theory has been incorporated into gender schema theory, which suggests that as children we develop a framework of knowledge—a gender schema—about what we think males and females typically do, and we then use that framework to interpret new information about gender.

3.3   Gender Socialization: Who Teaches Us How to Act Male or Female?
- Three theories suggest we learn gender behavior mainly from our environment.
- We are influenced by our parents, with fathers and mothers socializing their children differently according to what their own gender is.
- We are influenced by our peers, or those of equal status in age, class and the like.
- We are influenced by our teachers, who may subtly influence how boys and girls are more different than they are similar.
- We are influenced by the world of work, observing which occupations are dominated by males and which by females.

3.4   Gender Roles in Transition: Multiple Masculinities & Femininities
- The central feature of the traditional male role is instrumental—the focus is on work identity—which leads to higher income.
- The central feature of the traditional female role is expressive—the focus is on expressing tender feelings and being concerned with other's needs.
- For males the drawbacks are that their personal self-worth is tied to job position and income.
- For females, the drawbacks of the traditional gender roles are that they have reduced income and career fulfillment.
- Gender roles are changing as a result of the influence of the women's movement and the men's movement. The women's movement reflects feminism, the view that women should have the same economic, social, and political rights as men.
- The men's movement has divisions. Profeminists, the liberal branch, believe that a system of patriarchy forces all males into restrictive roles. Antifeminists, the conservative branch, believes that male dominance is natural. Masculinists agree the patriarchal system causes oppression but are concerned about males achieving self-realization.
- Trying to achieve a new gender role can lead to role conflict, the anxiety and confusion that occur when the expectations of two or more roles are incompatible.

Chapter Outline

- This chapter considers the vocabulary needed to be able to discuss gender intelligently. We also describe the four principal theories offered to account for gender differences. We then consider the key influences that, in addition to the media, influence our gender behavior: parents, peers, teachers, and the workplace. Finally, we consider the benefits and drawbacks of traditional gender roles and how gender roles are changing.

3.1 UNDERSTANDING GENDER & GENDER ROLES

Major Question: What are the principal terms anyone needs to know to discuss gender differences intelligently?

    a.   How to Talk about Gender: The Vocabulary

        i.   Sex: refers to the biological characteristics with which we were born that determine whether we are male or female.

        ii.   Gender: refers to the socially learned attitudes and behaviors associated with being male or female.

        iii.   A role is the behavior expected of someone who holds a particular status. A gender role is the behavior expected of a female or a male in a particular culture. A sex role is the behavior defined by biological constraints

        iv.   Socialization: the process by which people learn the characteristics of their group. Gender identity: is a person's psychological sense of whether he or she is male or female.

        v.   Cross-dresser: when a member of one gender dresses up in clothes, wigs, to appear to be a member of the other gender. Transvestite: usually a male cross-dresser, who dresses provocatively in order to appeal to men.

        vi.   Transsexual: a person with the biological sex of one gender who has the identity of the other gender and undergoes medical procedures to change to that gender. Transgenderist: a person with the biological sex of one gender who has the identity of the other gender, lives the full-time life of that gender but does not undergo medical procedures to change to that gender.

    b.   The Vocabulary of Sexism

        i.   Patriarchal: meaning male-dominated, male-identified, and male-centered societies. Matriarchal: means female-dominated, female-identified, and female-centered.

        ii.   Sexism: unjust discrimination based on a person's sex or the belief that one sex is innately superior to the other. Sexual harassment: the abuse of one's position of authority to force unwanted sexual attention on another person.

3.2 WHY DO GENDER ROLES DIFFER? SOME THEORIES

Major Question: What are some possible explanations for gender differences?

a.   Sociobiology: Does Biology Determine Our Gender Differences?

      i.   Sociobiology suggests that our social behavior—and gender behavior—results from biological differences. Men and women have the same sex hormones but men usually have more testosterone and women have more estrogen and progesterone.

b.   Social Learning Theory: Does the Environment Determine Our Gender Differences?

      i.   Social learning theory suggests we learn attitudes and behaviors through our interactions with the environment.

      ii.   We learn by reinforcement: desirable behavior is rewarded, and undesirable behavior is punished.

      iii.   We learn by modeling: while growing up we imitate the same-sex characteristics of parents, adults, other children, and the mass media personalities.

c.   Cognitive Development Theory: Does Our Age Determine Our Gender Differences?

      i.   Cognitive development theory suggests that the way we learn depends on our age.

d.   Gender Schema Theory: Do We Develop Mental Categories for Organizing Our Gender Perceptions?

      i.   Gender schema theory suggests that as children, we develop a framework of knowledge—a gender schema—about what we think males and females typically do, and we then use that framework to interpret new information about gender.

3.3 GENDER SOCIALIZATION: WHO TEACHES US HOW TO ACT MALE OR FEMALE?

Major Question: Who has influenced how I feel about being a man or woman?

a.   How Our Parents May Have Influenced Us

      i.   How Fathers & Mothers Treat Their Children Differently.

          1.   Fathers tend to spend more time with sons than daughters, and their attention may take the form of giving gifts or money.

          2.   Mothers tend to express affection and give verbal praise to daughters and sons equally.

      ii.   Four Ways Parents Socialize Their Children

          1.   By using different physical and verbal manipulations

          2.   By directing attention toward certain stereotypical gender-identified objects

          3.   By applying different verbal descriptions

          4.   By encouraging or discouraging certain stereotypical gender-identified activities.

      iii.   Differences in Class, Ethnicity, & Religion

b. How Our Peers May Have Influenced Us
   i.   How Girls Are Influenced
      1.   Girls influence other girls to play with toys that emphasize domesticity, nurturing, passivity, imagination, and emotional expression.
   ii.   How Boys Are Influenced
      1.   Boys influence other boys to play with toys that tend to emphasize logic, following rules, competition, and aggressiveness.
c. How Teachers May Have Influenced Us
   i.   How Teachers Influence Boys
      1.   Boys tend to get more attention from teachers than girls do, at all levels from nursery school to college.
   ii.   How Teachers Influence Girls
      1.   Girls do better than boys academically through elementary school, but boys catch up in middle school. Girls are less likely to be called upon by teachers than boys and receive less help with incorrect answers.
d. How Work May Influence Us
   i.   Occupations Dominated by Females
      1.   In general, about half of working women are found in one of two types of occupations: administration support and service support
   ii.   Occupations Dominated by Males
      1.   Men are dominant in construction, engineering, farming, law, medicine, scientists, professors, politics and religion.

3.4 GENDER ROLES IN TRANSITION: MULTIPLE MASCULINITIES & FEMININITIES

Major Question: Is there more than one way to be masculine or feminine?

a. The Benefits of Traditional Gender Roles
   i.   Benefits to Males: higher incomes and other job-related advantages; less domestic work and marital stress.
   ii.   Benefits to Females: identity tied to relationships rather than work; closer attachments with children.
b. The Drawbacks of Traditional Gender Roles
   i.   Drawbacks for Males: personal self-worth being tied to job position and income; job-related stress; less time for family life; limited emotional expression; limitations on child custody when divorced.
   ii.   Drawbacks for Females: reduced income and career fulfillment; dependence on the spouse, resulting in unhappiness; the beauty problem; less personal self-worth.

c. Changing Gender Roles
    i. The Women's Movement
        1. Liberal feminism—inequality rooted in sexism; is principally concerned with promoting individual rights and equal opportunities for women through legal and social reform.
        2. Socialist feminism—sexual division of labor rooted in class conflict; maintains that sexual division of labor and gender inequality is an expression of class conflict.
        3. Radical feminism—inequality rooted in patriarchy; considers male oppression to be the cause of female inequality.
        4. Lesbian feminism—oppression rooted in dominance of heterosexuality.
        5. Conservative feminism—promotes a return to traditional gender and family roles.
    ii. The Men's Movement
        1. Profeminists: agree with feminist women that patriarchy benefits white heterosexual males.
        2. Antifeminists: believe that male dominance is natural and therefore women's attempts to attain gender equality must be resisted.
        3. Masculinists: agree that the patriarchal system causes oppression and isolation but are more concerned with males' trying to achieve self-realization and self-expression.
d. Role Conflict, Androgyny, & Postgender Relationships
    i. Anxiety & Confusion: The Effects of Role Conflict
        1. Role conflict occurs when the expectations of two or more roles are incompatible.
    ii. Androgyny: Achieving Flexibility
        1. Androgyny is the quality of having in one person the characteristics of both males and females.
    iii. Postgender Transcendence: Beyond Gender
        1. Some male-female couples have abandoned notions that gender is destiny and reject gender as an ideological justification for inequality.
e. What Do You Want?
    i. In an egalitarian relationship, both partners pursue careers but also take care of the house and any children—on an equal basis.

Key Terms

Androgyny: the quality of having in one person the characteristics, as culturally defined, of both males and females. p. 98

Cognitive developmental theory: how children think, understand, and reason changes as they grow older, the result of biological maturation and increasing social experience.   p. 86

Cross-dressers: when a member of one gender dresses up in clothes, wig, and so on to appear to be a member of the other gender. p. 80

Feminism: the view that women should have the same economic, social, and political rights as men have. p. 96

Gender identity: a person's psychological sense of whether he or she is male or female. p. 80

Gender role: the behavior expected of a female or male in a particular culture, the attitudes and activities that a society expects of each sex. p. 79

Gender schema theory: suggests that as children, we develop a framework of knowledge—a gender schema—about what we think males and females typically do, and we then use that framework to interpret new information about gender. p. 86

Gender stereotype: the belief that men and women each display traditional gender-role characteristics. p. 86

Gender: refers to the socially learned attitudes and behaviors associated with being male or female. p. 79

Hormones: chemical substances secreted into the bloodstream by the endocrine glands. Men usually have more testosterone and women have more estrogen and progesterone. p.84

Matriarchal: societies that are female-dominated, female-identified, and female-centered. p. 83

Modeling: in social learning theory, the kind of learning attained through imitation of others. p. 85

Patriarchal: societies that are male-dominated, male-identified, and male-centered. p.82

Patriarchy: describes social arrangements in which positions of power and authority are mostly held by men. p. 97

Role conflict: occurs when the expectations of two or more roles are incompatible. p. 98

Role: the behavior expected of someone who holds a particular status. p. 79

Sex role: the behavior defined by biological constraints. For example, only women can give birth, and only men can be sperm donors. p. 79

Sex: refers to the biological characteristics with which we were born that determine whether we are male or female. p. 78

Sexism: unjust discrimination based on a person's sex or the belief that one sex is innately superior to the other. p. 83

Sexual harassment: the abuse of one's position of authority to force unwanted sexual attention on another person. p. 83

Social learning theory: suggests that we learn attitudes and behaviors through our interaction with the environment. p. 85

Socialization: the process by which people learn the characteristics of their group—the attitudes, values, and actions that are thought appropriate for them. p. 80

Sociobiology: suggests that our social behavior—and gender behavior—results from biological differences.

Transgenderist: a person with the biological sex of one gender who has the identity of the other gender, lives the full-time life of that gender but does not undergo medical procedures to change to that gender. p. 81

Transsexual: a person with the biological sex of one gender who has the identity or self-concept of the other gender and undergoes medical procedures to change to that gender. p. 80

Transvestite: usually a male cross-dresser who dresses provocatively in order to appeal to men. p. 80

Key People

Friedman, Betty: noted feminist writer of *The Feminine Mystique.*

Kohlberg, Lawrence: noted psychologist known for his work in cognitive developmental theory.

Piaget, Jean: noted Swiss psychologist known for his work in cognitive developmental theory.

Practice Test

1. On music videos, such as MTV, women:
    A. are shown to be aggressive problem solvers
    B. are shown as sex objects
    C. are shown as roles as housewife, reporter, nurse
    D. are shown as rescuing others from dangerous situations

2. Stereotypes:
    A. are accurate ways of seeing different types of people
    B. are views only held by the lesser educated working class of people
    C. are exaggerated expectations about a category of people
    D. serve a culture by helping individuals group types of people

3. The word "sex" refers to:
    A. biological characteristics that determine our being male or female
    B. anatomical differences such as genitals, breasts, etc.
    C. differences in sex chromosomes, hormones, and physiology
    D. all of the above

4. Gender refers to:
    A. the socially learned attitudes & behaviors of being male or female
    B. behavior expected of someone who holds a particular status
    C. behavior expected of a female or male in a particular culture
    D. behavior defined by biological constrains

5. Socialization:
    A. is the behavior defined by biological constraints
    B. is behavior expected of someone who holds a particular status
    C. is the process by which people learn the characteristics of their group
    D. is socially learned attitudes and behaviors of being male or female

6. Gender identity:
    A. is a person's psychological sense of whether he or she is male or female
    B. is a diagnosis for people who feel a desire to be the opposite sex
    C. is the behavior expected of a female or male in a particular culture
    D. is socially learned attitudes associated with being male or female

7. A transgenderist is:
    A. a cross-dresser who dresses provocatively to appeal to men
    B. when one gender dresses up in clothes to appear to be of the other gender
    C. a person who undergoes medical procedures to change their gender
    D. a person of one gender who has the identity of the other gender

8. Sexual harassment includes:
   A. suggestive remarks
   B. unwanted touching
   C. sexually oriented posters or graffiti
   D. all of the above

9. In regards to the concept of "Sexism" all of the following are true EXCEPT:
   A. in China parents often abort a fetus if they know it is a girl
   B. is defined as unjust discrimination based on a person's sex
   C. the belief that one sex is innately superior to the other
   D. is the abuse of one's authority to force unwanted sexual attention on another

10. Sociobiology suggests
   A. that hormones are not related to male and female behavior
   B. that our social behavior results from biological differences
   C. learning occurs through reinforcement and modeling
   D. we learn attitudes through interaction with the environment

11. Cognitive development theory, as understood by psychologist Jean Piaget, suggests:
   A. our gender behavior results from biological differences
   B. we learn behaviors through interaction with the environment
   C. children think, understand, and reason differently as they grow older
   D. that children learn through imitation of others

12. Gender schema theory suggests:
   A. we develop a framework of knowledge about male & female behavior
   B. that men and women display traditional gender-role characteristics
   C. that children at different stages handle gender identity differently
   D. the importance of observable behavior over internal feelings

13. Parents tend to socialize their children differently according to what their gender is, for example, fathers:
   A. spend more time with their sons than with their daughters
   B. set higher standards of accomplishments for their daughters
   C. tend to express affection to their sons and daughters equally
   D. tend to stress feelings in their relationships more with their sons

14. Parents subtly socialize their children in all of the following ways EXCEPT:
   A. by using different physical and verbal manipulations
   B. by applying different verbal descriptions to the same behavior
   C. by encouraging certain stereotypical gender-identified activities
   D. by clearly explaining the benefits of traditional gender roles

15. Teachers subtly influence gender behavior by:
    A. giving boys more attention than the girls
    B. calling on girls more often in class
    C. giving girls more time to talk when called upon
    D. expecting boys to work less at finding answers to problems

16. The central feature of the traditional male role is:
    A. expressive
    B. instrumental
    C. disciplinary
    D. provisionary

17. The primary drawback of traditional gender roles for females is:
    A. reduced income and career fulfillment
    B. personal self-worth being tied to job position and income
    C. job-related stress
    D. less time for family life

18. In the women's movement, Betty Friedan is best known for:
    A. being a Profeminist
    B. writing the book, *The Feminine Mystique*
    C. supporting the principles of patriarchy
    D. unifying the many viewpoints of modern feminism

19. In the women's movement, liberal feminism's primary concern is:
    A. inequality rooted in sexism
    B. sexual division of labor rooted in class conflict
    C. oppression rooted in dominance of heterosexuality
    D. inequality rooted in patriarchy

20. Androgyny is:
    A. not being competitive at times and nurturing at other times
    B. being illogical in one situation and emotional in another
    C. having in one person the characteristics of both males and females
    D. having the instrumental characteristics of traditional masculinity

21. Postgender transcendence is:
    A. enhancing the sexual experience with the spiritual dimension
    B. a relationship characterized as beyond gender
    C. embracing the notion that gender is destiny
    D. defining male success as being a good breadwinner

22. The men's movement includes all of the following EXCEPT:
    A. Antifeminists
    B. Masculinists
    C. Profeminists
    D. Prefeminists

23. In terms of the evolutionary goal of perpetuating the species, sociobiologists say:
    A. men seek mates that are more apt to be fertile
    B. women seek mates who are apt to make them feel loved
    C. men naturally value the aesthetics of a beautiful woman
    D. women prefer masculine dominance over security

24. In terms of gender differences, males:
    A. make up more than 90% of people with eating disorders
    B. account for 80% of all high school dropouts
    C. make up 82% of elementary school teachers
    D. make up 92% of bookkeepers and clerks

25. Stopping sexual harassment may involve:
    A. not being afraid of embarrassing the harasser
    B. contacting an appropriate authority if harasser doesn't stop
    C. tell the harasser in clear terms what behavior to stop
    D. all of the above

Project Suggestions

Project 1
Talk to your grandparents or older people and ask them what were the expected gender roles when they were growing up. What did you notice that has changed? What has stayed the same?

Project 2
Go to *www.childrennow.org* website. Scroll to Media Now and read about the current issue. What observations can you make about the differences in gender roles in the media?

Project 3
Look again at the viewpoints in the women's movement and the men's movement on pages 96–97. Which viewpoints do you agree with? Which ones do you disagree with? Why?

Answer Key

1. B (p.77)	6. A (p.80)	11. C (p.86)	16. B (p.93)	21. B (p.99)
2. C (p.76)	7. D (p.81)	12. A (p.86)	17. A (p.95)	22. D (p.97)
3. D (p.78)	8. D (p.82)	13. A (p.88)	18. B (p.96)	23. A (p.85)
4. A (p.79)	9. D (p.83)	14. D (p.88)	19. A (p.96)	24. B (p.83)
5. C (p.80)	10. B (p.84)	15. A (p.91)	20. C (p.98)	25. D (p.82)

Chapter 4

LOVE:

The Many Faces

Learning Objectives

At the end of the chapter, you ought to be able to answer the following questions:
1. What is love, and what are its two principal forms?
2. What are the principal theories on the origins of love?
3. What are three ways in which love can go away?
4. What distinguishes immature love from mature love?

Chapter Summary

4.1   Can We Define Love?
- Love can be defined as intimacy with, caring for, and commitment to another person. The portrayal of love in films, popular songs, television, and books helps to define and influence one's ideas about love.
- The meaning of love is subjective and can vary according to time, place, and culture.
- More important to the ancient Greeks were altruistic love (agape) and friendship love (philo). Passionate love was seen as unreliable, and as a result, marriages were arranged marriages with partners determined not by the bride or groom themselves but by their families.
- These views on arranged marriages influenced Europe in the Middle Ages, where great care was taken to make sure marriages would produce strong alliances of wealth and power.
- Between the 7th and 12th centuries, the Roman Catholic Church promoted marriage as a sacrament. The notion of courtly love became more and more accepted in society.
- Arranged marriages still exist in many parts of the world. Cultures vary greatly in their views on affection and how it should or should not be shown.
- As the United States became more industrialized choosing a marriage partner shifted from having an economic basis to emotional one.
- Love can have both a physical state, referred to as lust or sexual arousal, and a psychological state, or sexual desire.
- Friendship, an attachment between people, is the foundation for a strong love relationship. Friends enjoy each other's company, are willing to support and help

each other. Love involves emotional highs and lows, instability, passion, exclusiveness, and sexual desire.

- Although same-sex couples experience love with the same intimacy and intensity as any heterosexual couple, the way men and women express love as genders are more different than relationships between heterosexual and homosexual couples.

4.2   The Origins of Love: Some Theories
- The biochemical theory suggests that love results from our biological, chemical, and hormonal makeup.
- The attachment theory suggests our primary motivation in life is to be connected with other people for security.
- The wheel theory of love suggests that love develops and is maintained through rapport, self-revelation, mutual dependency, and intimacy need fulfillment.
- The triangular theory of love emphasizes three important elements of love that interact with one another: intimacy, passion, and decision/commitment.

4.3   The Dark Face of Love: Jealousy, Unrequited Love & Attempts to Control
- Jealousy occurs when you feel that something is threatening your relationship; it is a negative response to a real or imagined threat to a love relationship.
- Unrequited love, love that is not returned, is also a common negative aspect of love.
- Love can also go awry as a result of one person trying to control the behavior of the other. The attempts to control can include manipulation, stalking, and emotional and physical abuse.

4.4   How Can You Tell Whether It's Meaningful Love?
- Maturity in a love relationship is characterized by energy, meaning, self-esteem, no ghosts, and kindness.
- In meaningful love, partners tend to be trustworthy and stable, caring and kind, and likeable.

Chapter Outline

- In this chapter we consider the concept of soul mate and different definitions of love—particularly romantic love and companionate love. We also describe five theories of love: biochemical, attachment, wheel, triangular, and love styles. We look at what happens when loves goes away—jealousy, unrequited love, and attempts to control.

4.1   CAN WE DEFINE LOVE?
Major Question: What is love, and what are its two principal forms?
a.   Is Love All about Finding a Soul Mate?   A soul mate is a person who is temperamentally suited to another.

i.   Love Actually: Love is intimacy with, caring for, and commitment to another person. It arises from need satisfaction, sexual attraction, and/or personal or kinship ties.

ii.   Love in Other Times & Places

    1.   The ancient Greeks and Romans viewed passionate love as a kind of dangerous illness. Marriages were arranged by parents.

    2.   The Greek/Roman attitudes about love influenced Europe in the Middle Ages. Care was taken to make sure marriages would produce strong alliances of wealth and power.

    3.   During the 12th century there emerged the notion of courtly (or romantic) love—a preoccupation with and longing for union with a beloved.

    4.   India, China, Japan, and parts of Africa have histories of arranged marriages, which continues to today.

b.   Romantic Love & Companionate Love. Two anthropologists found evidence of passionate love in 147 or 166 societies they studied. They concluded that romantic love is a human, universal, or at the least a near-universal phenomenon.

i.   Romantic Love: More Than Lust?

    1.   Sexual desire, it is hypothesized, is the essential ingredient of romantic or passionate love.

ii.   Companionate Love: Intimacy, Affection, & Commitment

    1.   Companionate love, calmer than romantic love, emphasizes intimacy with, affection for, and commitment to another person.

c.   Friendship & Love

i.   Friendship is an attachment between people and is the basis for a strong love relationship. Although love relationships are based on friendship, there is more: Love involves emotional highs and lows, instability, passion, exclusiveness, and sexual desire—all qualities that are unstable.

d.   Same-Sex Love

i.   Same-sex couples experience love with the same intimacy and intensity as heterosexual couples; they often hide their true feelings because of public disapproval.

4.2   THE ORIGINS OF LOVE: SOME THEORIES

Major Question: What are the five principal theories on the origin of love?

a.   Biochemical Theory: Love is a Natural High

i.   The biochemical theory of love suggests that love results from our biological, chemical, and hormonal origins. The brains of passionate lovers release PEA (phenylethylamine), a natural amphetamine.

b.   Attachment Theory: Closeness Is a Survival Need

i.   The attachment theory of love suggests our primary motivation in life is to be connected with other people because it is the only security we ever have.

       1.   Secure adults find it not difficult to become friendly or intimate with others.

       2.   Avoidant adults are uneasy with being close to other people and with trusting and being dependent on them.

       3.   Anxious/Ambivalent adults are anxious their partners don't really love them or they won't stay with them.

c.   Wheel Theory: The Four Stages of Love

    i.   Stage 1: Rapport. Feelings of rapport are enhanced by similarities in social, cultural, and educational background and upbringing.

    ii.   Stage 2: Self-Revelation. Rapport leads to self-revelation, the disclosure of personal feelings.

    iii.   Stage 3: Mutual Dependency. Self-revelation leads to mutual dependency, the sharing of pleasures, ideas, humor, and sexual desires.

    iv.   Stage 4: Intimacy Need Fulfillment. You and your partner make mutual decisions, reinforce each other's goals, offer sympathy and support, and help each other satisfy deeper needs.

d.   Triangular Theory: Toward Consummate Love

    i.   The three components of love can be thought of as the corners of a triangle. The first component is intimacy, which is the warmth and bonding in a loving relationship.

    ii.   The second component is passion, which includes romance, physical attraction, and sexuality.

    iii.   The third component, decision/commitment, embodies one's decision to love someone and the commitment to love that person over time.

    iv.   A love relationship can vary in its combinations of intimacy, passion, and decision/commitment. The ideal combination is consummate love, when you and your partner's intimacy, passion, and decision/commitment are of the same intensity.

d.   Styles of Love: Lee's Six Kinds of Relationships

    i.   Love of Beauty & the Physical: Eros

    ii.   Obsessive Love: Mania

    iii.   Playful Love: Ludus

    iv.   Companionate Love: Storge

    v.   Altruistic Love: Agape

    vi.   Practical Love: Pragma

e.   Trying to Quantify Love: Is Intimacy the Foundation of Loving Relationships?

    i.   Researchers identified intimacy as consisting of, the presence of love and affection, the knowledge that someone loves and approves of us, being secure in the belief that one can disclose personal secrets, and willingness to reveal one's self.

4.3 THE DARK FACE OF LOVE: JEALOUSY, UNREQUITED LOVE, & ATTEMPTS TO CONTROL

Major Question: What are three ways in which love can go away?

a. Jealousy: The Green-Eyed Monster. Jealousy is defined as a usually intolerant or even hostile emotional response to a real or imagined threat to a love relationship.
  i. Jealousy: How It Works
    1. Jealousy sets boundaries for a relationship
    2. Jealousy may be either suspicious or reactive
  ii. Characteristics of Jealousy
    1. Men are jealous about sex, women about intimacy
    2. Men and women generally have different reactions
    3. Jealous people are more apt to be insecure people
    4. Jealousy isn't always just about sex, but it often is
    5. Jealousy is more prevalent in some cultures than others
b. Unrequited Love: When Love Is Not Returned
  i. More Attractive Rejects Less Attractive
  ii. Less Serious Rejects More Serious
c. Controlling: Trying to Control the Love Object
  i. Manipulation: From Charm to Threats
  ii. Stalking: Unwanted Following
  iii. Violence: Emotional or Physical Abuse

4.4 HOW CAN YOU TELL WHETHER IT'S MEANINGFUL LOVE?

Major Question: What distinguishes immature love from mature love?

a. Immature versus Mature Love
  i. Immature love is characterized in passionate thinking, passionate feeling, and passionate behavior.
  ii. Mature love is characterized by qualities of being trustworthy, stable, caring, kind, and someone you actually like.
b. The Concept of Soul Mate Revisited
  i. Once the emotional high of the initial passion is past, the greatest rewards of love come from approaching it rationally.

Key Terms

Agape: altruistic, unselfish, self-sacrificing love. p. 118

Arranged marriages: marriage partners determined not by the bride or the groom themselves but by their families. p. 108

Attachment theory of love: suggests that our primary motivation in life is to be connected with other people because it is the only security we ever have. p. 114

Biochemical theory of love: suggests that love results from our biological, chemical, and hormonal origins. p. 113

Companionate love: is calmer than romantic love, emphasizes intimacy with affection for, and commitment to another person. p. 111

Eros: the love of beauty, characterized by intense emotional attachment and powerful sexual feelings. p. 117

Friendship: an attachment between people and the basis for a strong love relationship. p. 111

Immature love: is passionate or romantic love characterized by passionate thinking, passionate feeling, passionate behavior. p. 124

Jealousy: a usually intolerant or even hostile emotional response to a real or imagined threat to a love relationship. p. 120

Lee's six styles of love: suggests there are six styles of love: love of beauty and the physical, obsessive, playful, companionate, altruistic, and practical. p. 117

Love: the intimacy with, caring for, and commitment to another person. p.107

Ludus: casual and carefree love that focuses on sex as recreational and not serious. p.118

Mania: obsessive love consisting of strong sexual attraction, emotional intensity, extreme jealousy, and mood swings between ecstasy and despair. p.118

Mature love: companionate love characterized by being trustworthy, stable, caring, kind and it is with someone you actually like. p. 125

Pragma: practical love that makes a rational assessment of a potential partner's positives and negatives. p. 119

Reactive jealousy: when evidence is revealed of a past, present, or anticipated relationship with another person. p. 121

Romantic love: an emotionally intense, passionate love in which a person believes that there is love at first sight, that there is only one true love, and that love conquers all. p. 108

Soul mate: a person who is temperamentally suited to another—one's best friend, confidant, and romantic partner. p. 106

Stalking: is repeatedly pursuing and frequently harassing another person. p. 122

Storge: affectionate, peaceful, and companionate kind of love. p. 118

Suspicious jealousy: occurring when there is no evidence or only ambiguous evidence for suspecting a partner is involved with someone else. p. 121

Triangular theory of love: emphasizes three important elements of love that interact with one another; intimacy, passion, and decision/commitment. p. 116

Unrequited love: love that is not returned. p. 122

Wheel theory of love: suggests that love develops and is maintained through four stages: rapport, self-revelation, mutual dependency, and intimacy need fulfillment. p. 115

Key People

Ainsworth, Mary: noted researcher of the attachment theory of love.

Gordon, Sol: North Carolina psychologist and sex educator who has written about mature and immature love.

Lee, John Alan: Canadian sociologist who proposed the six styles of love theory.

Reiss, Ira: noted sociologist who proposed the wheel theory of love.

Sternberg, Robert: researcher and writer who proposed the triangular theory of love.

Practice Test

1. For modern Americans, says anthropologist Charles Lindholm, romantic love:
    A. is seen as an essential human need
    B. is highly overrated
    C. is a mature notion
    D. is an immature notion

2. A soul mate is:
    A. a literary device manufactured to increase romantic novel book sales
    B. someone temperamentally suited for another
    C. someone 94% of never-marrieds believe they will never find
    D. an irrational fiction coming from Europe in the Middle Ages

3. According to the text, when does romantic love die?
    A. romantic love never dies, it just grows deeper
    B. it varies with every couple truly in love
    C. six to thirty months into a relationship it changes to companionate love
    D. approximately in the seventh year (the seventh year itch)

4. According to one survey in the text, how many people loved without being loved in return?
    A. 12%
    B. 45%
    C. 32%
    D. 75%

5. When it comes to defining "love":
    A. it is easily defined
    B. love is so overarching a notion as to defy definition
    C. can easily be found in the glossary of any marriage and family textbook
    D. has been precisely defined by sociologists

6. The ancient Greeks and Romans viewed passionate love:
    A. as the very essence of life itself
    B. the social sport of only the young and unmarried
    C. as a kind of dangerous illness
    D. as working against the inner journey of the spirit

7. Europe in the Middle Ages saw love as:
    A. a business and social arrangement
    B. an essential part of any marriage
    C. something only the wealthy could engage in
    D. a preserver of family stability

8. Many single people in India, China, and Japan prefer to have their parents pick their spouse because:
    A. their dowry is much larger then
    B. surveys show they lack the confidence needed to decide for themselves
    C. they believe arranged marriages are more stable than love-based marriages
    D. they are afraid of being socially ostracized

9. Recent sex surveys indicate that modern lovers believe kissing:
    A. is really quite secondary to intercourse
    B. is one of the most essential aspects of a relationship
    C. is to be of little interest to the modern female
    D. is to be as equally satisfying for the male as the female

10, Lust is:
    A. sexual arousal, the physical state of getting "turned on"
    B. a psychological state
    C. essential for passionate love
    D. is not to be distinguished from sexual desire

11. According to the text, with companionate love, lovers notice each other's:
    A. inner beauty
    B. spiritual characteristics
    C. imperfections
    D. A.Q., or affection quotient

12, Online dating services are limited for all of the following EXCEPT:
    A. people meeting online showcase their good points
    B. online life and real life aren't the same
    C. online connections can be emotionally intense
    D. the shear numbers of possible compatible matches is overwhelming

13. According to the biochemical theory of love, the "natural high" of being newly in love is:
    A. psychosomatically induced
    B. as powerful a stimulant as amphetamines and cocaine
    C. has no potentially addictive potential
    D. associated with the loss of desirable gene combinations

14. In terms of the attachment theory of love, adults who are uneasy with being close to other people and with trusting and being dependent on them, are classified as:
    A. Avoidant
    B. Secure
    C. Anxious/Ambivalent
    D. Anxious/Avoidant

15. According to sociologist Ira Reiss the last stage of the wheel theory of love is:
    A.   self-revelation
    B.   intimacy need fulfillment
    C.   rapport
    D.   mutual dependency

16. In the wheel theory of love mutual dependency is understood to mean:
    A.   you and your partner help each other satisfy deeper needs
    B.   the sharing of pleasures, ideas, humor, and sexual desires
    C.   the disclosure of personal feelings
    D.   the feeling of ease that makes you comfortable with each other

17. In the triangular theory of love fatuous love is:
    A.   love in which passion may have faded so that only commitment remains
    B.   love at first sight with overwhelming emotional involvement
    C.   foolish love, going from meeting to marriage in lightning speed
    D.   the love of good friends with no passion or commitment

18. According to Canadian sociologist John Alan Lee "Eros" is:
    A.   casual and carefree
    B.   altruistic, unselfish, self-sacrificing
    C.   obsessive, mood swings from ecstasy to despair
    D.   intense emotional attachment and powerful sexual feelings

19. According to the text, in a study of 360 undergraduate students scholars found that, compared to men, women:
    A.   place more emphasis on love, affection, and emotional sharing
    B.   are ambivalent in their feelings toward emotional intimacy
    C.   felt too much self-disclosure was intimidating and frightening
    D.   proved to be more accomplished at kissing

20. You go to a party with your lover; who then spends a lot of time talking to someone else. Afterward, you have a big fight about it. What's going on here?
    A.   your love is not being returned, it is a feeling of unrequited love
    B.   one person is trying to control the behavior of the other
    C.   you feel something is threatening your relationship, you're jealous
    D.   you are feeling the pain of the more attractive rejecting the less attractive

21. According to the text, love can go awry when one person tries to control the behavior of the other, using tactics including all of the following EXCEPT:
    A.   stalking
    B.   spying
    C.   manipulation
    D.   violence

22.   According to the text, immature love is most characterized by:
      A.   passionate thinking
      B.   the enjoyment of many sexual partners
      C.   strong sexual attraction, with jealousy, and mood swings
      D.   making irrational assessments of a partner's positives and negatives

23.   What most adults between 30 and 54 say they are looking for in a mate:
      A.   passionate behavior
      B.   good grooming, good health, and similar age
      C.   financial security
      D.   good mental health and spiritual maturity

24.   According to psychologist Sol Gordon the qualities you need to consider to determine whether you are a good candidate for love include:
      A.   no ghosts, that is, not allowing the past to haunt you
      B.   passionate feeling
      C.   romantic love
      D.   a willingness to bypass friendship for love

25.   According to the text, once the emotional highs of the initial passion is past, the greatest rewards of love come from approaching it:
      A.   with an open heart
      B.   rationally
      C.   intuitively
      D.   spiritually

Project Suggestions

Project 1
Like to know how romantic you are? Complete the "Romantic Experience Survey" at *www.people.umass.edu/mvernon/consent2.htm* What did you learn about yourself?

Project 2
Complete the Self-Assessment: How Capable Are You of Being Intimate? on page 126 of the text. Ask your best friend to complete it as well. Talk about what you learned.

Project 3
Ask five fellow students what do they really mean when they tell someone "I love you." What kind of responses did you get? Was this a difficult question for some people? Why?

Answer Key

1. A (p.105)	6. C (p.108)	11. C (p.111)	16. B (p.115)	21. B (p.122)
2. B (p.106)	7 A (p.108).	12. D (p.112)	17. C (p.117)	22. A (p.119)
3. C (p.107)	8. C (p.109)	13. C (p.113)	18. D (p.117)	23. B (p.123)
4. D (p.107)	9. B (p.110)	14. A (p.114)	19. A (p.119)	24. A (p.123)
5. B (p. 107)	10. A(p.110)	15. B (p.115)	20. C (p.120)	25. B (p.125)

Chapter 5 INVOLVEMENT:

Dating, Pairing, Courtship, & Cohabitation

Learning Objectives

At the end of the chapter, you ought to be able to answer the following questions:
1. Why date? What functions can it serve for me?
2. How can I find someone to love?
3. Why might I live together with someone, and what would it be like?
4. How do people react to a deteriorating relationship, and how can I handle a breakup?

Chapter Summary

5.1 The Dating Game
- Courtship, the process by which a commitment to marriage is developed, was the major way in which people went about establishing a relationship before the eras of serial dating and cohabitation.
- Closed courtship, or arranged marriage, is evident in blind marriages, in which neither partner sees the other until the day of their wedding. It is also evident in marriages that involve a bride price, in which a man pays money or property to the bride's family.
- Today's courtship system is an open system and is a relationship or marriage market in which prospective partners compare the personal, social, and financial resources of eligible mates and bargain for the best they can get.
- Dating is the process of meeting people socially for the purpose of possibly forming an exclusive long-term relationship.
- Some scholars believe that in an attempt to find a suitable mate, people find one another more desirable on the basis of homogamy, or similarity in education, ethnicity, race, religion, age, and social class.

5.2 Pairing Up: Finding & Choosing a Partner
- Finding and choosing a partner can be influenced by the type of setting in which one interacts. Open fields are settings in which people do not normally interact. Closed fields are settings in which people are likely to interact.
- Although most people meet through personal introductions, others are making use of classified ads, meeting online, and introduction services.

- Traditional courtship evolves from dating to going steady to engagement to marriage.
- Dating arrangements in college vary from just hanging out to hooking up (physical encounters that allow possible sexual interaction without commitment) to couples spending all their time together.
- With an average workweek of 47 hours, Americans have great opportunities to interact with and possibly date fellow employees.
- For many people, dating is a second-time-around experience in which they find themselves as a single parent or after a divorce or death of a spouse.

5.3   Cohabitation: Living Together as an Unmarried Couple
- Cohabitation, or living together, is defined as a couple in an emotional and sexual relationship sharing living quarters without being married.
- The primary reasons for cohabiting include security, emancipation from parents, convenience, and as a testing mechanism to determine whether marriage might be workable.
- Cohabitants tend to have similarities in independence, sex, attitudes, religion, income, and education.
- Cohabitation has increased in the United States as a result of increased social tolerance, increased female equality, and views of many people as to the impermanence of marriage.
- Cohabitants are expected to support themselves, frequently maintain financial independence, and might not follow traditional gender roles in performing housework.
- Cohabitation offers partners a time to test the relationship, companionship with independence, and greater ease in ending the relationship.
- Couples who are considering living together should consider how well they know each other, why they are moving in together, how they will manage money, the similarities of their preferred lifestyles, their feelings on children and parenting, and legal issues such as wills and health-care proxies.

5.4   Breaking Up Is Hard To Do
- When relationships start to deteriorate, people may have several responses. The neglect response is characterized by avoidance and neglect. The exit response involves ending the relationship. The loyalty response involves partners staying together without working on the relationship, hoping that things will improve. The voice response involves identifying the problems and working to save the relationship.
- In a breakup, it is important to consider whether you can accept that the pain of rejection is natural, identify what steps you can take to stop thinking about the other person, and focus on what you can do to raise your self-esteem.

Chapter Outline

- We first consider courtship, both closed and open systems; six functions of dating; and how dating can operate as a filtering process. Next we describe four ways of meeting people and variations in dating. We then discuss cohabitation and why people live together, their characteristics, why living together has increased, and how it differs from marriage. Finally, we discuss aspects of a deteriorating relationship and breaking up.

5.1   THE DATING GAME

Major Question: Why Date? What functions can it serve for me?

a.   Courtship: From Parental Decisions to the Relationship Marketplace
  i.   The Closed Courtship System: Arranged Marriages
    1.   In times past, and in many cultures still, courtship was a closed system: children's marital destiny was decided by their parents.
  ii.   The Open Courtship System
    1.   Western nations have an open courtship system, in which we make our own decisions about choosing our partners.
b.   The Functions of Dating
  i.   Recreation: dating can be, or is supposed to be fun.
  ii.   Companionship: dating is a way of having friends
  iii.   Intimacy & Sex: many teens discover sex and sexuality in the course of dating
  iv.   Mate Selection: a goal for many in dating is to find a mate
  v.   Socialization: dating helps to socialize us to get along with the opposite sex
  vi.   Status Achievement: dating enhances a person's status by showing others that he or she is acceptable, desirable, or grown up
c.   Is Dating a Filtering Process?
  i.   Types of Filtering: Propinquity, Endogamy, Exogamy
    1.   Propinquity: you filter people on the basis of their nearness to you in time and place
    2.   Endogamy: you filter people on the expectation you marry within your own social group, race, religion, social class
    3.   Exogamy: you filter people on the cultural expectations that you marry outside your family group, to avoid incest
  ii.   Factors Affecting Availability: Race, Class, Age, Religion
    1.   Traditionally, race has been a strong factor in influencing dating, living-together, and marriage patterns. However, interracial dating seems to be becoming more acceptable.
    2.   People tend to date and mate with people from their own social class.
    3.   People tend to marry within their own age range.
    4.   As many as 90% of people who get married do so with people who have similar religious values.

iii. One Dating Model: A Three-Stage Filtering Process
  1. The first stage involves physical attraction.
  2. In the second stage people compare their values.
  3. In the third stage, the two negotiate role compatibility.
iv. Another Dating Model: Is Commitment Relationship-Driven or Event-Driven?
  1. Some dating couples go through a filtering process with the two growing in their commitment as they sort out their mutual preferences, values, goals, and roles.
  2. Other couples go through an event-driven process of swinging back and forth between commitment and ambivalence, often quite dramatically.
v. Close Dating Relationships & Personal Growth
  1. A longitudinal study concluded that the supportive assistance that individuals received from their dating partners and the love the partners reported for them indeed predict the growth that the individual later experienced.

5.2 PAIRING UP: FINDING & CHOOSING A PARTNER

Major Question: How can I find someone to love?
a. Finding a Partner Amid Masses of People
  i. Open Fields: Interaction Unlikely
    1. Open fields are settings in which people do not normally interact and so potential partners are not likely to meet.
  ii. Closed Fields: Interaction Likely
    1. Closed fields are settings in which people are likely to interact and so potential partners may meet.
b. Meeting People
  i. Personal Introductions
    1. Between one-third and one-half of dating relationships begin with a personal introduction.
  ii. Classified Ads
    1. Personal classified ads are a popular way to meet people interested in dating, mating, or sex.
  iii. Meeting Online
    1. Relationship websites take personal classified ads to another level by offering an opportunity to meet a partner online.
  iv. Introduction Services
    1. Introduction services do much the same thing as print and Internet dating ads, the services offering (for a fee) to introduce people to each other.
c. Variations in Dating
  i. Traditional Courtship: From Dating to Engagement
    1. Traditionally a sequence of meeting, dating, going steady, proposal, engagement, and marriage was followed.
  ii. On Campus Today: Hanging Out, Hooking Up, & Joined at the Hip

1. Hanging out: spending time in unstructured groups together, or students socializing in unpartnered groups.
2. Hooking up: a physical encounter that allows sexual interaction—ranging from kissing to having sex—without commitment.
3. Joined at the hip: the opposite of hanging out or hooking up, in which the two people do everything together with each other— eat, study, do laundry, and sleep together.
  iii. Dating in the Workplace
1. Americans now work an average of 47 hours a week, often in work teams and joint projects, which provides more opportunity for office dating.
  iv. Second-Time-Around Dating
1. For the single parent, the divorced, the widowed, and singles over 65, dating has special challenges, especially if the person has children.

5.3 COHABITATION: LIVING TOGETHER AS AN UNMARRIED COUPLE

Major Question: Why might I live together with someone, and what would it be like?
a. People Who Live Together: Why & Who
  i. Four Reasons for Cohabiting
1. The Linus blanket: one partner is highly insecure or dependent and prefers any relationship to no relationship.
2. Emancipation: one or both partners enter into a relationship to express independence from their parents' values about sexuality.
3. Convenience: two partners get their needs fulfilled without benefit of a traditional marriage.
4. Testing: a couple lives together in a kind of trial marriage, to find out whether getting married would probably work for them.
  ii. Cohabitation Nation: Who Are the Live-Togethers?
1. They are more independent.
2. They have more sexual experiences and sex more often.
3. They are more liberal, including views on gender roles.
4. They are slightly less religious.
5. They have a slightly lower income.
6. They tend to be lower in education.
  iii. Why Living Together Has Increased
1. Social tolerance: many people regard sex between two people as permissible behavior.
2. Female equality: woman are now more economically self-sufficient.
3. Impermanence of marriage: high divorce rates make marriages seem a less permanent arrangement.

b.   The Experience of Living Together
     i.   Three Stages of Living Together
         1.   Year 1—Blending: partners are infatuated with each other.
         2.   Year 2 & 3—Nesting: as passion subsides, the partners. emphasize other grounds for compatibility
         3.   Year 4 & 5—Maintaining: the partners establish patterns of stability and traditions.
     ii.   Some Differences between Marriage & Living Together
         1.   Work: the two cohabiting partners are expected to individually support themselves.
         2.   Finances: cohabiting partners maintain their financial independence.
         3.   Housework: in cohabiting relationships the woman does not spend as much time on housework.
     iii.   The Advantages of Living Together
         1.   Relationship test: couples can see how workable their future together might be.
         2.   Companionship with independence: cohabitation provides a sexual partner and companionship plus independence.
         3.   Easier termination: with fewer legal entanglements it is easier to end the relationship than a marriage.
     iv.   The Disadvantages of Living Together
         1.   Lack of commitment: couples are less apt to stay faithful and to work through problems.
         2.   Exploitation: a woman might be asked to pay half of expenses even though her income may be less.
         3.   Fewer legal rights: unless agreements are made by legal contract ending a relationship can be full of hassles.

5.4   Breaking Up Is Hard to Do

Major Question: How do people react to a deteriorating relationship, and how can I handle a breakup?

a.   Four Ways of Reacting to a Deteriorating Relationship
     i.   The Neglect Response: Just Let the Relationship Go Ahead & Fall Apart
     ii.   The Exit Response: We Have to End Our Relationship
     iii.   The Loyalty Response: Let's Just Stick It Out Despite Any Difficulties
     iv.   The Voice Response: We Need to Talk about Improving Our Relationship
b.   Ending a Relationship
     i.   If Your Partner Breaks Up with You
         1.   Can you accept that the pain of rejection is natural?
         2.   What steps can you take to stop thoughts about the other person?
         3.   What can you do to raise your self-esteem?

  ii. If You Break Up with Your Partner
    1. Are you really sure you want to break up—that the relationship can't be improved?
    2. Can you be honest and accept that your partner will be hurt?
    3. Can you put off "just being friends" and terminate the relationship completely?

Key Terms

Blind marriage: a marriage in which neither partner saw the other until the day of their wedding. p. 133

Bride price: a man must pay money or property to the future bride's family for the right to marry her. p. 133

Closed fields: settings in which people are likely to interact and so potential partners may meet. p. 140

Cohabitation or living together: couple living in an emotional and sexual relationship without being married. p. 149

Courtship: the process by which a commitment to marriage is developed. p. 132

Dating: the process of meeting people socially for the purpose of possibly forming an exclusive long-term relationship. p. 134

Dowry: the money, property, or goods a woman brings to the marriage. p. 133

Elope: when a couple run away and marry apart from their parents. p. 133

Endogamy: you filter people on the basis of the cultural expectation that a person marries within his or her own social group in terms of race, religion, and social class. p. 136

Engagement: a period of time that begins with the marriage proposal and a formal announcement that the couple plans to be married. p. 147

Exit response: the resolution of withdrawing or threatening to withdraw from a relationship. p. 157

Exogamy: you filter people on the basis of the cultural expectations that a person marries outside your family group and not practice sex with siblings. p. 136

Homogamy: marriage between partners of similar education, ethnicity, race, religion, age, and social class. p. 136

Hooking up: a physical encounter that allows possible sexual interaction—ranging from kissing to having sex—without commitment. p. 148

Loyalty response: a passive but constructive response consisting of choosing to stay with one's partner despite any problems but making no attempt to try to resolve them, hoping they will smooth out over time. p. 157

Mail-order brides: businesses that specialize in publishing profiles and photos women mainly for the benefit of American men seeking wives. p. 146

Marriage bureaus: businesses that arrange social introductions for a fee. p. 146

Marriage squeeze: one sex has a more limited pool of eligible marriage candidates than the other. p. 138

Mating gradient or marriage gradient: refers to the tendency for men to marry downward in class and women to marry upward with respect to age, education, and occupational success. p. 138

Neglect response: a destructive reaction that tends to occur when a person is not much invested in the relationship, doesn't want to deal with any problems in it, and is willing to let the partnership simply wither away. p. 156

Open fields: settings in which people do not normally interact and so potential partners are not likely to meet. p. 140

POSSLQs: a term that stands for "People of the Opposite Sex Sharing Living Quarters." p. 149

Propinquity: you filter people on the basis of their nearness to you in place and time. p. 136

Relationship market or marriage market: a system in which prospective partners compare the personal, social, and financial resources of eligible mates and then bargain for the best they can get. p. 134

Socialization: the process by which we learn the skills we need to survive as individuals and as members of society. p. 135

Status: the social ranking, or the prestige attached to a particular position in society. p. 135

Video dating services: a dating service where you are allowed to watch videotapes of others talking and in various activities in return for allowing others to watch your tape. p. 146

Voice response: the choice of people who value the relationship and who are invested in it but who feel that it has problems that need to be discussed. p. 157

Key People

Phillips, Deborah: author of the book *How to Fall Out of Love.*

Rusbult, Caryl: scholar who developed the *exit-voice-loyalty-neglect model*; which deals with four ways people typically try to deal with deteriorating relationships.

Solot, Dorian & Miller, Marshall: founders of the Alternatives to Marriage Project, and authors of *Unmarried to Each Other: The Essential Guide to Living Together.*

Whitehead, Barbara Dafoe: co-director of the National Marriage Project at Rutgers University.

Practice Test

1. Speaking of the contemporary movement in dating and mating, sociologist Andrew Cherlin says:
    A. our culture has never been healthier
    B. we have lost the ability to slow down the process of becoming intimate and choosing a partner
    C. we continue to have the assistance of parents and elders in the community
    D. rules about dating and mating are clear and certain

2. A study of the heterosexual dating culture of 1,000 college women at 11 four year American colleges found that about _____ of the women respondents reported having had at least one "hook up" (sex without commitment) and ____ had had more than six.
    A. 40%, 10%
    B. 20%, 5%
    C. 80%, 20%
    D. 60%, 15%

3. One study found that the primary reason cohabiting college students break up is:
    A. they graduated and moved away from each other
    B. their parents strong disapproval
    C. too many differences and different values
    D. they got tired of arguing and fighting

4. In closed courtship systems where marriages are arranged, the dowry:
    A. is the price a man must pay to the brides family in order to marry her
    B. is when the couple runs away and is married away from the parents
    C. is when neither partner sees the other until their wedding day
    D. is the money or goods a woman brings to the marriage

5. In open courtship systems where you choose your own partner, the relationship market is:
    A. the activity of comparing personal resources and bargaining for the best
    B. people seeking exclusively their one true soul mate
    C. intentionally spending time in public looking for a mate
    D. single's bars where people seek sexual or dating partners

6. Dating has all of the following functions EXCEPT:
    A. companionship
    B. intimacy & sex
    C. mate selection
    D. propinquity

7. In the filtering process of dating, exogamy is:
   A. marriage between partners of similar backgrounds
   B. the cultural pressure to marry outside your family group
   C. the cultural expectation to marry within a group, race, or religion
   D. the process of dating and mating those near you in place and time

8. The primary element encouraging partners to seek each other out and marry is:
   A. same race
   B. same religion
   C. personality characteristics
   D. similar socioeconomic status

9. According to a 1997 Gallup/*USA Today* poll of 602 teenagers ages 13–19, _____ of those who had been out on dates said that they had dated someone from a different racial or ethnic group.
   A. 9%
   B. 57%
   C. 93%
   D. 18%

10. One aspect of dating and mating within social class is the mating gradient, which is:
    A. the opposite of the marriage gradient
    B. the tendency for men to marry upward and women downward
    C. the tendency for men to marry downward in class and women upward
    D. the prestige attached to a particular position in society

11. One aspect of dating and mating in regards to age is the marriage squeeze, which is:
    A. the process by which we learn social skills as we mature
    B. the pressure our culture puts on us to marry within our social group
    C. when one sex has a more limited pool of eligible candidates than the other
    D. the pressure our culture puts on men to marry downward in social class

12. When it comes to religion, as many as _____ of people who get married do so with people who have similar religious values.
    A. 90%
    B. 13%
    C. 47%
    D. 60%

13. One dating model has a three-stage filtering process; the third and final stage of that process is:
    A. when the two people compare their individual values
    B. when the two people are attracted to each other physically
    C. when the two people negotiate compatibility roles
    D. when the two people accept each others personality characteristics

14. When it comes to finding a partner amid masses of people it is best to look:
    A. in open fields
    B. in closed fields
    C. in playing the field
    D. in the field of opportunity

15. People meet people in all kinds of ways, all of the following are common ways EXCEPT:
    A. meeting online
    B. classified ads
    C. chance encounters
    D. personal introductions

16. One type of introduction service is a Marriage Bureau, which:
    A. arranges introductions for a fee
    B. publishes profiles and photos of women for men seeking wives
    C. allows you to watch videotapes of potential dates or mates
    D. allows you 8 minutes to interview 8 potential date/mates

17. On college campuses today students use the term "hooking up," which means:
    A. spending time in unstructured groups together
    B. a physical encounter that allows possible sexual interaction
    C. two people doing everything with each other
    D. studying for computer courses in small groups

18. As many as _____ Americans enter into a romance with a fellow employee each year.
    A. 500,000
    B. 2 million
    C. 8 million
    D. 13 million

19. Currently about _____ Americans live with unmarried partners of the opposite sex according to the 2000 census.
    A. 9.6 million
    B. 3.2 million
    C. 17.7 million
    D. 22.1 million

20. In the U.S. people who live together before marriage have the following characteristic compared to those who don't live together before marriage:
    A. they are slightly more religious
    B. they have slightly higher incomes
    C. they tend to be lower in education
    D. they are more dependent

21. In the three stages of living together model, the term "blending" refers to:
    A. when the partners are infatuated with each other
    B. when the partners deemphasize sex and seek deeper compatibility
    C. when the partners establish patterns of stability and traditions
    D. when the partners work to include their families of origin

22. According to researcher Scott Stanley men who cohabit with the woman they eventually marry are:
    A. more committed to the marriage than men who don't cohabit before marriage
    B. less committed to the marriage than men who don't cohabit before marriage
    C. more committed to the institution of marriage
    D. ambivalent about the idea of a life-long marriage

23. According to scholar Caryl Rusbult's exit-voice-loyalty-neglect model of deteriorating relationships, the neglect response is:
    A. Let's just stick it out despite any difficulties
    B. We need to talk about improving our relationships
    C. Just let the relationship go ahead and fall apart
    D. We have to end our relationship

24. One study of college students found that _____ of women and _____ of men had experienced the breakup of at least one relationship.
    A. 93%, 95%
    B. 88%, 89%
    C. 72%, 77%
    D. 69%, 47%

25. According to the text, for some people, the painful breakup of a love relationship can lead to:
    A. love addiction
    B. obsessive/compulsive behavior
    C. manic/depressive episodes
    D. permanent isolation

Project Suggestions

Project 1

Compared to married couples live-togethers don't have as deep a commitment toward each other during their time together. They are aware that the relationship could be ended at any time. Do you know of any cohabiting couples who have been together for 10 years or more? Interview them to find out how and why they have stayed as a cohabiting couple. What did you learn?

Project 2

If you were to submit a personal ad to a newspaper or the internet what safety precautions would you take? Compare your thoughts with the Practical Action Box ideas on page 144. What other points would you add?

Project 3

What do think the advantages and disadvantages are in the college student behavior of "hooking up" (a physical encounter that allows possible sexual interaction)? What would your parents, grandparents, and siblings have to say about this practice?

Answer Key

1. B (p.131)	6. D (p.135)	11. C (p.138)	16. A (p.146)	21. A (p.153)
2. A (p.133)	7. B (p.136)	12. A (p.138)	17. B (p.148)	22. B (p.155)
3. C (p.133)	8. C (p.136)	13. C (p.139)	18. C (p.148)	23. C (p.156)
4. D (p.133)	9. B (p.136)	14. B (p.140)	19. A (p.150)	24. B (p.157)
5. A (p.134)	10. C (p.138)	15. C (p.141)	20. C (p.152)	25. A (p.158)

Chapter 6 SEXUALITY:

Interpersonal Sexuality, Sexual Values, & Behavior

Learning Objectives

At the end of the chapter, you ought to be able to answer the following questions:
1.   How did I learn to think what I think about sex?
2.   What are all the forms of sexual expression?
3.   How could having sex risk my health and my life?

Chapter Summary

6.1   Sexual Values, Learning, & Scripts
- Sexual values are deeply held beliefs and attitudes about what is right and wrong, desirable and undesirable sexual behavior.
- Many of the sexual values people acquire come from various forms of the media. Unfortunately, these sources of sexual values lack factuality and are distortions of the nature of sex, sexual roles, and treat women as sex objects.
- In today's society, premarital sex and nonmarital sex are more accepted than they were 50 years ago.
- Besides the effect of the media, sources of sexual values and beliefs include, parents, religion, siblings and peers, sex education programs, and sex partners.
- Sex scripts are the interpretations and behaviors we have learned from society and others that are expected of us in sexual situations.

6.2   The Varieties of Sexual Experience
- Until the 1940s the study of sex was considered off-limits. Research by Alfred Kinsey, Masters and Johnson, and Helen Singer Kaplan led to the development of a five-stage model—desire, arousal, plateau, orgasm, and resolution—of sexual response for men and women.
- Sexual expression runs along a continuum of behaviors and involves both thoughts and actions. A sexual fantasy is any mental representation of any kind of sexual activity. Sexual fantasies can act as a safe outlet for people without partners.
- Masturbation, which is practiced both by people in relationships and by people who are not, is self-stimulation of the genitals for sexual pleasure. The practice is

not considered abnormal unless it interferes with one's life or with enjoyable sexual sharing in a relationship.

- Foreplay or sex play may or may not lead to sexual arousal and intercourse. Kissing, touching, and genital play are examples of foreplay and may involve the touching or kissing of erogenous or sexually sensitive areas. Sexual acts that do not involve the exposure to semen, vaginal secretions, or blood are referred to as outercourse.
- Oral-genital stimulation consists of mouth-to-genital contact to stimulate sexual pleasure.
- Sexual intercourse, also referred to as coitus, involves the penetration of the vagina by the penis and is the only sexual act that can achieve procreation.
- Individuals may also practice celibacy—either complete celibacy, with no sex at all, or partial celibacy, involving masturbation but no sexual relations with others.
- Pornography and prostitution are referred to as commercialized sex.
- Deviance is relative, varies from place to place, and changes over time. Five specific types of atypical sexual behavior are voyeurism, fetishism, exhibitionism, sadomasochism, and obscene phone calls.
- Though the media are guilty of promoting and depicting unrealistic views of sex, real-life sexual difficulties occur and include, inhibited sexual desire, sexual addiction, erectile dysfunction, inability to have an orgasm, dyspareunia, and vaginismus.

6.3   AIDS, Other Sexual Diseases, & Safer Sex
- Love and passion may lead people to take chances and possibly engage in risky sexual behavior, possibly resulting in a person's contracting an infectious disease or even a life-threatening virus.
- The most serious types of illness that can be transmitted through sexual contact are the human immunodeficiency disease (HIV) and acquired immune deficiency syndrome (AIDS).
- HIV/AIDS can be detected through the use of tests. Even though there is no cure for HIV and AIDS, there are a number of drugs used in the treatment that can slow the progress of the disease and increase the survival rate.
- Sexually transmitted diseases caused by viruses cannot be cured. Sexually transmitted diseases caused by bacteria can be cured.
- Reducing the risks of acquiring STDS can be facilitated by consistently using safer-sex measures such as condoms and spermicide and by avoiding the use of alcohol and other drugs that may cloud one's judgment.
- The safest kind of sex avoids the exchange of semen, vaginal secretions, saliva, or blood. This can be accomplished through saved sex or abstinence, which is the voluntary avoidance of sexual intercourse.
- A condom is a thin sheath made of latex rubber or lamb intestine that keeps the semen from being transmitted to a man's sex partner and shields against contact with any infection on the penis.
- A dental dam that is designed for use in dental surgery is a flat 5-inch piece of latex that is place over the vaginal opening and surrounding area. It is used by

females who are the recipient of oral sex to prevent the exchange and
transmission of bodily fluids.
- High-risk sexual behaviors include unprotected sex and any behavior that
  involves sharing intravenous needles.

Chapter Outline

- In this chapter we discuss sexual values, learning, and scripts. Then we describe the
  varieties of sexual experience and include a short discussion about sexual dysfunctions.
  The final section describes HIV/AIDS, other sexually transmitted diseases, and safer sex.

6.1   SEXUAL VALUES, LEARNING, & SCRIPTS

Major Question: How did I learn to think what I think about sex?

  a. Sexual Values

      i.   Four Standards of Premarital & Nonmarital Sex

          1.   The double standard—the standard according to which
premarital or nonmarital sex is more acceptable for men
than for women.

          2.   Permissiveness with affection—allows premarital or
nonmarital sex for both women and men, provided that they
have an affectionate and committed relationship.

          3.   Permissiveness without affection—allows premarital or
nonmarital sex for women and men regardless of the amount or
affection or stability in their relationship.

          4.   Abstinence—the voluntary avoidance of sexual intercourse.

      ii.   Sexual Values of College Students

          1.   Absolutism—people who adhere to strict codes, usually based
on religion, that dictate what is right and wrong.

          2.   Hedonism—people who believe, "If it feels good, do it, but
don't hurt anybody in the process."

          3.   Relativism—people who believe "what you do sexually
depends on the person you are with, how you feel about each
other, and the nature of the relationship."

      iii.   Age of First Intercourse

          1.   6.6% of 2001 high school students had had sexual intercourse
before age 13, but by the 12th grade, 60.5% had.

  b.   How We Learn about Sex

      i.   The Influence of Parents

          1.   Most parents hold back in discussing sex because they are
afraid they will embarrass their teenagers, will be asked
questions they can't answer, or will impel their teens into
becoming sexually active if they give them too much
information.

          2.   Most teens are reluctant to discuss sex with their parents
because of embarrassment, belief that their parents are "old-

fashioned," fear that they will be asked personal questions, or a wish not to shock or upset their parents
    ii.   The Influence of Religion
        1.   Direction influence—the strength of religious beliefs and frequency of church attendance are related to the delay of first intercourse.
        2.   Indirect influence—the more religious a person is, the less drinking he or she is apt to do, and lower alcohol consumption is related to lower frequency of risky sexual behavior.
    ii.   The Influence of Friends & Siblings
        1.   Friends, not parents, are the most important source of information about sex and influences on teenager's sexual values and on a teen's decision to become sexually active.
    iii.   The Influence of Sex Education
        1.   Sex education programs in high schools generally seem to have a positive influence on teenagers' knowledge about sex but they have not been found to influence teens' sexual attitudes or behaviors.
    iv.   The Influence of Sexual Partners
        1.   Once one becomes involved with sexual partners, they become the most important factor in modifying our sexual expectations.
  c.   Sexual Scripts
    i.   A sexual script is a set of expectations as to how one should behave in sexual situations.
        1.   Men's sexual scripts—men are supposed to be in charge, confident, and aggressive, not tender and compassionate. The purpose of sex is orgasm rather than intimacy.
        2.   Women's sexual scripts—women are expected to be beautiful, loving, nurturing, and accommodating. Unlike men, they are not supposed to talk about sex or to be overly interested in sex.

6.2 THE VARIETIES OF SEXUAL EXPERIENCE

Major Question: What are all the forms of sexual expression?
  a.   The Human Sexual Response
    i.   Excitement—the excitement phase consists of a physical reaction to erotic stimulation, whether thought, touch, taste, sight, and/or sound.
    ii.   Plateau—during the plateau phase, sexual excitement and muscle tension continue to build.
    iii.   Orgasm—the orgasmic phase is the most ecstatic for those who experience it. Rhythmic contractions cause the release of neuromuscular tension and feelings of intense pleasure.
    iv.   Resolution—the resolution phase is the return of the body to its unaroused state.
  b.   The Different Kinds of Sexual Behavior
    i.   Sexual Fantasies & Dreams

      1.   A sexual fantasy is any mental representation of any kind of sexual activity.

      2.   A sexual dream occurs during sleep, without a person's conscious control, and may produce a nocturnal orgasm, an involuntary orgasm during sleep.

  ii.   Masturbation

      1.   Masturbation is self-stimulation of the genitals for sexual pleasure resulting in orgasm.

  iii.   Kissing, Touching, & Genital Play

      1.   Foreplay is stimulating activity that might or might not culminate in sexual intercourse.

  iv.   Oral-Genital Stimulation

      1.   Oral-genital stimulation consists of mouth-to-genital contact to stimulate sexual pleasure.

  v.   Anal Stimulation

      1.   Anal intercourse consists of inserting the penis into the anus and is a sexual behavior engaged in by people regardless of sexual orientation. Anal sex is one of the riskiest activities for transmission of sexual diseases.

  vi.   Sexual Intercourse

      1.   Sexual intercourse means coitus, which involves penetration of the vagina by the penis.

  vii.   Celibacy

      1.   Celibacy may be complete—a person has no sex at all—or partial—a person masturbates but has no sexual relations with others.

  viii. Pornography & Prostitution

      1.   Pornography—is a depiction through words or pictures of sexual conduct involving opposite-sex or same-sex partners designed to cause sexual excitement.

      2.   Prostitution—is the exchange of sexual services for money or sometimes drugs.

  ix.   Atypical Sexuality

      1.   Forms of atypical sexual expression include voyeurism, fetishism, exhibitionism, sadomasochism, obscene phone calls.

c.   Sexual Difficulties & What to Do about Them

  i.   Inhibited Sexual Desire

      1.   Inhibited sexual desire (ISD) is a lack of interest in sex or an inability to feel sexual or get sexually aroused.

  ii.   Sex Addiction: Compulsive Sexual Behavior

      1.   Sexual addiction, or compulsive sexual behavior, is an intense preoccupation with sex. It makes having a satisfying sexual relationship with just one lover difficult.

  iii.   Sexual Dysfunctions In Men

      1.   Erection difficulties—erectile dysfunction, or impotence, is failure to achieve or maintain an erection.

2. Premature ejaculation—is a man's inability to reasonably control his ejaculatory reflex on a regular basis.
iv. Sexual Dysfunctions in Women
1. Inhibited female orgasm is a term that is now used instead of frigidity to describe an inability to reach orgasm.
2. Painful intercourse—painful or difficult sexual intercourse is call dyspareunia.
3. Involuntary spasms of vaginal muscles—known as vaginismus, involuntary spasms of the muscles surrounding the lower third of the vagina prevent the penis from entering.

6.3 AIDS, OTHER SEXUAL DISEASES, & SAFER SEX
Major Question: How could having sex risk my health and my life?
a. Sexually Transmitted Diseases
i. Sexually transmitted diseases are infectious diseases that are transmitted as a result of sexual contact.
b. HIV & AIDS: The Modern Scourge
i. AIDS stands for acquired immune deficiency syndrome, a sexually transmitted disease that is caused by a virus known as HIV.
ii. HIV, or human immunodeficiency virus, the virus causing AIDS, brings about a variety of ills, including the breakdown of the immune system.
iii. Who Gets HIV/AIDS ?
1. For AIDS-related deaths in the U.S. in 2002, about 52% were among blacks, 28% among whites, 19% among Hispanics, and less than 1% among Asians/Pacific Islanders and American Indians/Alaska Natives.
iv. How Do People Get Infected?
1. The people most at risk for HIV/AIDS are men who have sex with men, men and women who inject drugs, and men and women having heterosexual contact.
v. Heterosexuals with HIV/AIDS
1. The rate of heterosexual HIV transmissions is rising at three times the rate for homosexual transmission.
vi. Detecting HIV/AIDS
1. If you share needles or syringes to inject drugs or steroids or if you have had sex with someone whose sexual history you don't know or with numerous sex partners, you should consider being tested.
vii. Dealing with HIV/AIDS
1. At present, no vaccine is available to prevent or cure HIV or subsequent AIDS symptoms.
c. Other STDs
i. Reducing Risks of Acquiring STDs/Principles of Prevention
1. Use precaution universally—consistently use safer-sex measures with all partners

2. Keep your head clear—drugs cloud your judgment, placing you in a position of increased vulnerability
    ii. Lower Risk: "Saved" Sex, Including Abstinence
        1. Abstinence is the voluntary avoidance of sexual intercourse
        2. Saved sex is touching but avoiding all contact with body fluids
    iii. Somewhat Risky: "Safer" Sex, Including Use of Condoms
        1. The next best step to ensuring safe sex is to use latex: condoms and dental dams
    iv. Very Risky: Unprotected Sex & Other Behavior
        1. High risk behavior includes all forms of sex in which body fluids may be exchanged.
        2. High risk behavior includes sharing needles for intravenous injection of drugs, a prime means of transmitting STDs.
    v. Mutual Monogamy
        1. Having multiple sex partners is one of the leading risk factors for the transmission of STDs. Clearly, mutual monogamy is one way to avoid infection.

Key Terms

Abstinence: is the voluntary avoidance of sexual intercourse. p. 168

AIDS: stands for acquired immune deficiency syndrome, a sexually transmitted disease that is caused by a virus known as HIV. p. 185

Anal intercourse: consists of inserting the penis into the anus and is sexual behavior engaged in by people regardless of sexual orientation. p. 178

Anorgasmic: the inability to have an orgasm. p. 176

Celibacy: complete celibacy is when a person has no sex at all. Partial celibacy is when a person masturbates but has no sexual relations with others. p. 179

Condom (prophylactic or rubber): is a sheath of latex rubber or lamb intestine. p. 192

Cunnilingus: is oral stimulation of the clitoris, labia, and vaginal opening. p. 178

Dental dam: used by a female when receiving oral sex. It is a 5-inch-square piece of latex that is placed over the vaginal opening and surrounding area. p. 193

Double standard: the standard according to which premarital and nonmarital sex is more acceptable for men than for women. p. 168

Dyspareunia: painful or difficult sexual intercourse for women. A burning or sharp pain when the penis is inserted into the vagina. p. 183

Erectile dysfunction or impotence: is failure to achieve or maintain an erection. p. 182

Erogenous or sexually sensitive: areas of the body such as genitals, breasts, the anal area in some people that can lead to sexual excitement and even lead to orgasm when touched or kissed. p. 177

Excitement phase: consists of a physical reaction to erotic stimulation, whether thought, touch, taste, sight, and/or sound. p. 174

Exhibitionism: consists of exposing ("flashing") one's genitals in public to an involuntary observer, usually male to female. p. 180

Fellatio: is oral stimulation of the penis by a partner. p. 178

Fetishism: is behavior in which a person receives sexual arousal or pleasure from focusing on a nonsexual object or part of the body, such as a shoe or the foot. p. 180

Foreplay or sex play: is stimulating activity that might or might not culminate in sexual intercourse. p. 177

HIV: stands for human immunodeficiency virus, the virus causing AIDS, and brings about a variety of ills, including the breakdown of the immune system. p. 185

Impotence or erectile dysfunction: is failure to achieve or maintain an erection. p. 182

Inhibited female orgasm (frigidity): is a term used to describe the inability to reach orgasm. p. 183

Inhibited sexual desire (ISD): is a lack of interest in sex or an inability to feel sexual or get sexually aroused. p. 181

Masturbation: is self-stimulation of the genitals for sexual pleasure, as with one's hand or with a vibrator, resulting in orgasm. p. 177

Multiorgasmic: the ability to have multiple orgasms within a single period of sexual arousal. p. 176

Nocturnal orgasm: an involuntary orgasm during sleep. p. 176

Oral-genital stimulation: consists of mouth-to-genital contact to stimulate sexual pleasure. p. 177

Orgasmic phase: is the most ecstatic sexual phase consisting of rhythmic contractions cause the release of neuromuscular tension and feelings of intense pleasure. p. 175

Outercourse: is the name given to sexual acts that do not involve the exposure of a partner to semen, vaginal secretions, or blood. p. 177
p. 178

Permissiveness with affection: this standard allows premarital and nonmarital sex for both women and men, provided that they have an affectionate and committed relationship. p. 168

Permissiveness without affection: this standard allows premarital and nonmarital sex for both women and men, regardless of the amount of affection or stability in their relationship. p. 168

Plateau phase: during the plateau phase sexual excitement and muscle tension continue to build. Blood pressure and heart rate continue to rise, and breathing becomes faster. p. 175

Pornography: a depiction through words or pictures of sexual conduct involving opposite-sex or same-sex partners designed to cause sexual excitement. p. 179

Premature ejaculation: is a man's inability to reasonably control his ejaculatory reflex on a regular basis. p. 182

Procreation or reproduction: the result of sexual intercourse in producing a baby. p. 178

Prostitution: is the exchange of sexual services for money or sometimes drugs. p. 179

Resolution phase: the return of the body to its unaroused state. Heart rate, blood pressure, breathing, muscle tension, and nipple erection all subside. p. 176

Sadomasochism: involves deriving sexual pleasure from the infliction or receiving of pain. p. 180

Sexual addiction or compulsive sexual behavior: is an intense preoccupation with sex and makes having a satisfying sexual relationship with just one lover difficult. p. 181

Sexual fantasy: is any mental representation of any kind of sexual activity. p. 176

Sexual intercourse or coitus: sexual activity that involves penetration of the vagina by the penis. p. 178

Sexual response: a four-phase model of how both men and women respond to sex physiologically, consisting of (1) excitement, (2) plateau, (3) orgasm, and (4) resolution. p. 174

Sexual script: is a set of expectations as to how one should behave in sexual situations, whether male or female, heterosexual or homosexual. p. 173

Sexual values: are deeply held beliefs and attitudes about what is right and wrong, desirable and undesirable sexual behavior. p. 166

Sexually transmitted diseases (STDs): are infectious diseases that are transmitted as a result (usually) of sexual contact. p. 184

Vaginismus: involuntary spasms of the muscles surrounding the lower third of the vagina and prevent the penis from entering. p. 183

Voyeurism: is behavior in which one becomes sexually aroused by looking at people, often strangers, undressing or having sex without their being aware that they are being watched. p. 180

Key People

Kaplan, Helen Singer: researcher and writer on sexual behavior that added modified the Master and Johnson four-phase model of sexual response to include a "desire" stage.

Kilbourne, Jean: writer and researcher who compiled examples of media images and their effects on young people, especially women.

Kinsey, Alfred: pioneer researcher in the study of sex in the 1940s and 1950s.

Knox, David: sociologist who studied 620 never-married college students and identified three sexual values that guided their behavior in sexual decision making.

Masters, William, and Johnson, Virginia: pioneer sex researchers who developed a four-phase model of sexual response.

Reiss, Ira: sociologist who identified four values or societal standards about premarital sex.

Practice Test

1.   One survey found that _____ of adult Americans said television was their most important source of information about sex.
      A.   3%
      B.   11%
      C.   29%
      D.   48%

2.   In terms of media discussion of safer sex and contraception, a study of 50 episodes of various TV soap operas revealed, only _____ was there a mention of the risk of AIDS arising from unprotected sex.
      A.   twice
      B.   once
      C.   on five occasions
      D.   on four occasions

3.   A 1988 study of college students found that _____ of the women and _____ of the men had experienced unwanted sexual activity, including kissing, petting, and sexual intercourse.
      A.   49%, 3%
      B.   16%, 7%
      C.   97%, 93%
      D.   62%, 23%

4.   One of the reasons people go against their own wishes and give in to sexual activity is "Enticement," which is:
      A.   feeling obligated or not knowing what else to do
      B.   thinking that one needs to have the experience
      C.   satisfying the other person simply because he or she wants it
      D.   consisting of seductive acts by the other person, such as touching

5.   In terms of how often do people have sex, a study of married and unmarried adults reported:
      A.   once a week
      B.   three times a week
      C.   twice in a month
      D.   four times a week

6.   Sociologist Ira Reiss identified four values about sex, one of those values was the "double standard," which:
      A.   allows sex provided the partners have a committed relationship
      B.   allows sex as a recreational pursuit
      C.   allows men more sexual leeway than women
      D.   allows voluntary avoidance of sexual intercourse

7.   Sociologist David Knox identified three sexual decision making values of college students; one of those values was "absolutism," which:
     A.   adheres to strict codes, usually based on religion
     B.   is best described as, If it feels good, do it
     C.   suggests it all depends on the other person, the feelings, the relationship
     D.   are our deeply held beliefs about what is right and wrong

8.   In terms of age of first intercourse, a study of 2001 high school students showed ____ had had sexual intercourse by the twelfth grade.
     A.   10.3 %
     B.   27.7 %
     C.   60.5 %
     D.   89.6 %

9.   Most parents hold back on talking to their teenagers about sex for all the following EXCEPT:
     A.   they are afraid they will embarrass their teenager
     B.   they are afraid the teen will ask questions they can't answer
     C.   they are afraid too much information will impel the teen to sexual activity
     D.   they are afraid the teen cannot adequately understand

10. Sex-education programs in high school generally seem to have a _____ influence on teenagers' knowledge about sex.
     A.   negative
     B.   positive
     C.   neutral
     D.   mixed

11. As for being blond, a 1991 study reportedly found that ____ of American boys prefer blond females to brunets or redheads.
     A.   12%
     B.   60%
     C.   80%
     D.   94%

12. A sexual script:
     A.   is our deeply held beliefs about what is right or wrong
     B.   is our attitudes about desirable and undesirable sexual behavior
     C.   is a set of expectations as to how one should behave in sexual situations
     D.   is how men and women respond to sex physiologically

13.   In the Masters and Johnson four-phase model of sexual response, the plateau phase is:
       A.   rhythmic contractions causing intense pleasure
       B.   the return of the body to its unaroused state
       C.   a physical reaction to erotic stimulation
       D.   when sexual excitement and muscle tension continue to build

14.   In terms of the varieties of orgasms, the term "anorgasmic" means:
       A.   able to have multiple orgasms within a single period of sexual arousal
       B.   unable to have an orgasm
       C.   rhythmic contractions that cause release of neuromuscular tension
       D.   the clitoris, uterus, vagina, and vaginal lips return to their normal state

15.   In terms of different kinds of sexual behavior, the term "nocturnal orgasm" means:
       A.   an involuntary orgasm during sleep
       B.   any mental representation of any kind of sexual activity
       C.   the second of the two stages of male ejaculation
       D.   the clitoris swells, vaginal walls lubricate, & the uterus enlarges

16.   Masturbation:
       A.   is stimulating activity that might culminate in sexual intercourse
       B.   is self-stimulation of the genitals for sexual pleasure
       C.   is a sexual act that does not involve semen, vaginal secretions, or blood
       D.   is the penis becoming fully erect, and the testes swell and elevate

17.   Oral stimulation of the penis by a partner is known as :
       A.   cunnilingus
       B.   mutual oral-genital simulation
       C.   fellatio
       D.   outercourse

18.   One of the riskiest activities for transmission of sexual disease, including HIV, is:
       A.   the erogenous zone
       B.   anal intercourse
       C.   self-stimulation of the genitals for sexual pleasure
       D.   use of the dental dam

19.   Procreation:
       A.   are those favoring teaching creation in public schools
       B.   refers to reproduction
       C.   risks the exchange of bodily fluids and the passage of STDs
       D.   is oral stimulation of the clitoris, labia, and vaginal opening

20. According to the text, BDSM:
    A. consists of exposing one's genitals in public
    B. is becoming sexually aroused by secretly looking at people having sex
    C. derives sexual pleasure from the infliction or receiving of pain
    D. receiving sexual pleasure from focusing on a nonsexual object

21. In terms of sexual difficulties, inhibited sexual desire (ISD):
    A. is a lack of interest in sex or inability to feel sexual
    B. is an intense preoccupation with sex
    C. is failure to achieve or maintain an erection
    D. is masturbating but having no sexual relations with others

22. Dyspareunia:
    A. is involuntary spasms around the vagina preventing penis entry
    B. is a burning or sharp pain when the penis is inserted into the vagina
    C. is the inability for the female to reach orgasm
    D. is the inability to control the ejaculatory reflex on a regular basis

23. The STD known as "the great imitator" because its sores mimic those of other diseases is:
    A. pelvic inflammatory disease
    B. gonorrhea
    C. syphilis
    D. herpes

24. The text recommends that the best kind of condom is made of:
    A. natural membrane
    B. lambskin
    C. lamb intestine
    D. latex

25. The text recommends that when a female is the recipient of oral sex she should wear:
    A. a prophylactic
    B. a dental dam
    C. an IUD
    D. a female condom

Project Suggestions

Project 1

Go to the website for the Sexuality Information and Education Council of the United States, at *www.siecus.org* and ask all the questions you had about sex but were afraid to ask. Were you able to ask any questions that Siecus couldn't answer?

Project 2

What kind of sex education did you receive? Who was most influential: parents? friends? religion? sex partners? Evaluate who was most influential and why.

Project 3

For some people their religious beliefs play a large part in shaping their views on sex. How have your religious or spiritual views affected or not affected the way you think about sex and sexual behavior?

Answer Key

1. C (p.164)	6. C (p.168)	11. C (p.172)	16. B (p.177)	21. A (p.179)
2. B (p.165)	7. A (p.168)	12. C (p.173)	17. C (p.178)	22. B (p.183)
3. C (p.166)	8. C (p.169)	13. D (p.175)	18. B (p.178)	23. C (p.191)
4. D (p.166)	9. D (p.170)	14. B (p.176)	19. B (p.178)	24. D (p.194)
5. A (p.167)	10. B (p.171)	15. A (p.176)	20. C (p.180)	25. B (p.193)

Chapter 7   Marriage:

The Ultimate Commitment?

Learning Objectives

At the end of the chapter, you ought to be able to answer the following questions:

1. What are good and bad reasons for getting married, and what expectations do people have?
2. What four phases might a marriage go through, and how do they relate to marital satisfaction?
3. What are three ways in which I might classify marriage relationships?
4. What are the characteristics of successful marriages, and how could I achieve success in my own marriage?

Chapter Summary

7.1   Why Do People Marry?

- Marriage can be defined as a legal union between a man and a woman.
- Positive reasons for marrying include emotional security, companionship, and the desire to be parents.
- Negative reasons for marrying include physical attractiveness or emotional security; pressure from parents, peers, partners, or pregnancy; and escape, rebellion, rebound, or rescue.
- Marital expectations include: (1) undergoing certain rituals, as engagement, wedding ceremony, and honeymoon; (2) sexual exclusivity and permanence in relationship; and (3) making an important legal commitment.
- A rite of passage can be viewed as an event that signals a major change from one social status to another.
- In making a pledge of monogamous marriage, most partners assume that their relationship will be built around the promises of sexual exclusivity and permanence.
- Since marriage is a legal agreement the state has an interest in how you terminate the marriage and in how you divide property and share children if you divorce.
- A covenant marriage is an antidivorce contract in which couples demonstrate their strong commitment to marriage.
- A prenuptial agreement is a contract signed by the couple before the wedding that specifies in advance how property will be divided in the event of divorce or death.

- A postnuptial agreement is the same as a prenuptial agreement except that it is worked out by partners who are already married to each other.

7.2 Changes in the Family Life Cycle: Scenes from a Marriage
- Family life has four phases: (1) beginning, with perhaps the greatest marital satisfaction; (2) child rearing, often with less marital satisfaction; (3) middle age, with more marital satisfaction; and (4) aging.
- The beginning phase lasts about two to three years. Couples may experience the loss of independence, new friends and relatives, possible changes in career and domestic roles, and identity bargaining.
- The child rearing stage can be characterized by less marital satisfaction and consisting of five stages: childbearing, preschoolers, school children, adolescents, and child launching.
- The middle-age phase is normally time when the last child has left home and continues to retirement.
- The aging phase of marriage parallels the time when most income earners will be approaching retirement. Many people find this to be a time of adjustment to the new lifestyle and interaction with their spouse.

7.3 Different Kinds of Marriage Relationships
- Utilitarian marriages are marriages based on convenience and are of three types: (1) conflict-habituated marriage, (2) devitalized marriage, and (3) passive-congenial marriage.
- Intrinsic marriages are marriages that are inherently rewarding and are of two types: (1) vital, and (2) total.
- Wallerstein and Blakeslee proposed four types of "good marriages": romantic, rescue, companionate, and traditional.
- A study conducted by Kantor and Lehr suggested that there are three family systems: closed, open, and random.

7.4 What Makes for a Successful Marriage?
- Marital success, also called marital quality, is measured in terms of stability, happiness, and flexibility.
- Homogamous marriages are between partners of similar education, ethnicity, race, religion, age, and social class. Heterogamous marriages are those in which the partners are of different education, ethnicity, race, religion, age, and social class.
- Similar temperaments, shared interests, strong family ties on both partner's sides, and similar views on children are important in marital quality.
- The more income a couple has and the higher their occupational status, the more apt they are to say they have a good marriage.
- Two important factors in marital quality are equity (the partners give in proportion to what they receive) and equality (the partners have equal status).
- The first thing to realize is that marriage is a journey, not a destination, and that the journey should be its own reward. Mature love is based on commitment, acceptance and caring, and flexibility.

- Static marriages don't change over time, don't allow for changes in the spouses, and rely on the fact of the legal marriage bond to enforce sexual exclusivity and permanence.
- Flexible marriages allow the partners to change over time and to grow as individuals and in the relationship.

Chapter Outline

- We first discuss good and bad reasons for getting married, the expectations people have for marriage, and different marriage contracts. We then describe four phases in a family life cycle: beginning, child rearing, middle age, and aging. In the third section, we discuss three classifications for marriage relationships. Finally, we cover what makes for successful marriages.

7.1 WHY DO PEOPLE MARRY?

Major Question: What are good and bad reasons for getting married, and what expectations do people have?

    a.   Why Individuals Get Married

        i.   Common reasons for getting married are: we're in love, companionship, desire for children, and happiness

        ii.   Marriage for the Right Reasons

            1.   Emotional security—"I want to fill a vacancy within myself."

            2.   Companionship—"I want to love and be loved by someone else."

            3.   Desire to be a parent—"I want to have and raise children."

        iii.   Marriage for the Wrong Reasons

            1.   Physical attractiveness or economic security

            2.   Pressure from parents, peers, partners, or pregnancy

            3.   Escape, rebellion, rebound, or rescue

    b.   Happiness, Marriage, & Race: The Interracial Experience

        i.   Interracial Marriage: The Background

            1.   Black-white marriages were banned in the late 1600s, outlawed in the 18th century; the laws are now struck, yet as late as 1991, 66% of whites said they would oppose marriage with a black.

        ii.   Tolerance & Acceptance: Improved, but Could Be Better

            1.   Nearly half of black-white couples thought that marrying someone of a different race made marriage more difficult.

    c.   The Expectations People Have for Marriage

        i.   Marriage as Rite of Passage

            1.   Engagement—a couple's way of signaling to the world that they intend to marry.

            2.   Wedding—are at a minimum a civil event, involving the power of the state, require the couple to obtain a marriage license.

3. Honeymoon—its purpose is to allow the couple to recover from the stresses of the wedding and to begin to establish their new identity as legally wed husband and wife.

ii. Marriage in Expectation of Sexual Exclusivity & of Permanence
1. Sexual exclusivity—"Forsaking all others," each partner promises to have sexual relations only with the other.
2. Permanence—"So long as we both shall live," the partners promise to stay together lifelong.

iii. Marriage as a Legal Commitment
1. The covenant marriage contract—"We want to demonstrate a stronger commitment to our marriage."
2. The postnuptial agreement—"Because of new circumstances in our marriage, we now want to determine how property will be divided in the event of divorce."
3. The prenuptial agreement—"Before marriage, we want to determine how property will be divided in the event of divorce."

7.2 CHANGES IN THE FAMILY LIFE CYCLE: SCENES FROM A MARRIAGE

Major Question: What four phases might a marriage go through, and how do they relate to marital satisfaction?

a. Beginning Phase: Greatest Marital Satisfaction?
i. Identity Bargaining
1. The realities of the marriage oblige spouses to adjust to their idealized expectations of each other.

ii. Loss of Independence
1. Some free spirits find themselves frustrated by the responsibilities and confinements of marriage.

iii. New Friends & Relatives
1. Getting married means getting to know your partner's family members and friends.

iv. Career & Domestic Roles
1. The first year is when you work out your respective career and domestic responsibilities, allocation of living expenses, and division of household tasks.

b. Child-Rearing Phase: Less Marital Satisfaction?
i. Stages of Child Rearing
1. The five stages are: childbearing, preschoolers, school children, adolescents, and launching young adults.

ii. Changes During the Child-Rearing Years
1. Work—working parents may be stressed by the demands of commuting, job insecurity, low pay, and child-care demands.
2. Domestic—partners in a marriage have to negotiate sharing of domestic work—cooking, shopping, cleaning, laundry, and home maintenance.

        3.   Sex—frequency may decline but many report extreme physical pleasure with their partners.
- c. Middle-Age Phase: More Marital Satisfaction?
  - i. Improved Marital Satisfaction
    1. Without children in the house, the parents can begin to enjoy each other more.
  - ii. Lack of Marital Satisfaction
    1. If the couple are taking care of returned adult children or elderly relatives, the extra responsibilities can contribute to diminished marital satisfaction.
- d. Aging Phase
  - i. After 30 or 40 years of marriage, most income earners will be nearing retirement and this may require some adjustments.

7.3 DIFFERENT KINDS OF MARRIAGE RELATIONSHIPS

Major Question: What are three ways in which I might classify marriage relationships?

- a. Five Types of Enduring Marriages: Cuber & Harroff's Research
  - i. Utilitarian Marriages: Three Types of Unions Based on Convenience
    1. Conflict-habituated marriages—"We thrive on conflict."
    2. Devitalized marriages—"Our marriage is a lost cause, but we're resigned to it."
    3. Passive-congenial marriages—"Our marriage is based on practicality, not emotion."
  - ii. Intrinsic Marriages: Two Types of Inherently Rewarding Unions
    1. Vital marriages—"We really enjoy being together and sharing most of our lives."
    2. Total marriages—"We intensely enjoy being together and sharing every area of our lives."
- b. Four Types of "Good Marriages" & Their Built-in "Antimarriages": Wallerstein & Blakeslee's Research
  - i. The Romantic Marriage: "Our Passion Will Last Forever"
    1. The built-in seeds of destruction are that the partners are so preoccupied with each other that they neglect their children and the rest of the world.
  - ii. The Rescue Marriage: "We're Making Up for Our Past Unhappiness"
    1. Because husband and wife have wounded each other in the past, the relationship always allows the possibility for renewed strife based on earlier abuses.
  - iii. The Companionate Marriage: "We Have a Friendly, Egalitarian Relationship"
    1. If both spouses are too much involved in their respective careers, they might begin to spend less time with each other.
  - iv. The Traditional Marriage: "He's the Breadwinner, She's the Homemaker"

        1.   The possibility is that the spouses will become so involved in their traditional roles and responsibilities that all they have in common is their interest in the children.

    c.   Three Types of Family/Marriage Systems: Kantor & Lehr's Research
        i.   The Closed System: "We Value Tradition; the Family is Most Important"
            1.   This system values the family over the individual and emphasizes tradition, stability, belonging, and caring for each other.
        ii.   The Open System: "We Value Consent; Both the Family & the Individual Are Important"
            1.   This system is sensitive to both individual and family needs and tries to achieve consensus in ideas and feelings.
        iii.   The Random System: "We Value Freedom; the Individual Is Most Important"
            1.   This system focuses on the needs of individuals and tend to value freedom, intensity, and spontaneity.

    d.   What Can We Conclude?
        i.   None of the three classifications of marital/family relationships can be considered to reflect the North American population at large. The samples are too small.
        ii.   These marital/family models do not point to one kind being necessarily better than another.
        iii. None of the relationships described seems to suggest a recipe for a stable and happy marriage.

7.4   WHAT MAKES FOR A SUCCESSFUL MARRIAGE?

Major Question: What are the characteristics of successful marriages, and how could I achieve success in my own marriage?

    a.   Good Marriages: What the Research Shows
        i.   Similar Backgrounds: Homogamy
            1.   Marriages between partners of similar education, ethnicity, race, religion, age, and social class are more apt to be successful than heterogamous marriages.
        ii.   Commonalities: Similar Characteristics & Interests
            1.   Similar temperaments
            2.   Shared interests
            3.   Strong family ties on both sides
            4.   Similar views on children
        iii. Economic Status, Work, & Two-Paycheck Couples
            1.   Both working—spouses bring home their work frustrations, and guilt about not being full-time parents.
            2.   Both working—spouses have more income and may find their jobs satisfying thus improving their mental health.
        iv.   Domestic Work & Child Care: The Importance of Equity & Equality

1. Equity means that partners give in proportion to what they receive.
2. Equality means the partners have equal status.

b. Your Personal Journey to Marriage Success
   i. Commitment
      1. Couples in happy marriages see their union as a long-term commitment.
   ii. Acceptance & Caring
      1. Partners in happy marriages accept each other for what they are—as individuals and as "good friends."
   iii. Flexibility
      1. Static marriages don't change over time, don't allow for changes in the spouses, and rely on the fact of the legal marriage bond to enforce sexual exclusivity and permanence.
      2. Flexible marriages allow the partners to change over time and to grow as individuals and in the relationship.
   iv. Vow Renewals & Personal Marriage Agreements
      1. A vow renewal is a ceremony in which a couple repeat their commitment to each other.
      2. A personal marriage agreement is a written agreement negotiated between married couples in which partners specify how they will behave in aspects of the relationship.

Key Terms

Closed-type family or marriage: is one that values the family over the individual and emphasizes tradition, stability, belonging, and caring for each other. p. 222

Companionate marriage: the spouses base their relationship on equality and friendship. p.221

Conflict-habituated marriage: a marriage characterized by ongoing tension and unresolved conflict. p. 218

Covenant marriage: an antidivorce contract in which couples demonstrate their strong commitment to marriage. p. 209

Devitalized marriage: a marriage in which the partners have lost the strong emotional connection they once had but stay together out of duty. p. 219

Empty-nest syndrome: a feeling of depression after the children have moved out or "fled the nest." p. 216

Family life cycle: the stages of development in a family where member's roles and relationships change, largely depending on how they have to adapt themselves to the absence or presence of child-rearing responsibilities. p. 213

Flexible marriages: marriages that allow the partners to change over time and to grow as individuals and in the relationship. p. 226

Heterogamous marriages: marriages between partners of different education, ethnicity, race, religion, age, or social class. p. 223

Homogamous marriages: marriages between partners of similar education, ethnicity, race, religion, age, and social class. p. 223

Identity bargaining: the realities of the marriage oblige spouses to adjust their idealized expectations of each other. p. 213

Intrinsic marriages: marriages that are fundamentally rewarding. p. 219

Marital success or marital quality: a relationship measured in terms of stability, happiness, and flexibility. p. 223

Marriage: a legal union between a man and a woman. p. 202

Miscegenation: marriage or cohabitation between a white person and a person of another race. p. 205

Open-type family or marriage: is sensitive to both individual and family needs and tries to achieve consensus in ideas and feelings. p. 222

Passive-congenial marriage: a marriage in which the couple focus on activities rather than emotional intimacy. p. 219

Permanence: means that the partners promise to stay together lifelong. p. 209

Personal marriage agreement: a written agreement negotiated between married couples in which partners specify how they will behave in aspects of the relationship. p. 227

Postnuptial agreement: a contract signed by the couple after the wedding that specifies in advance how property will be divided and children cared for in the event of divorce or one partner's death. p. 212

Prenuptial agreement: a contract signed by the couple before the wedding that specifies in advance how property will be divided and children cared for in the event of divorce or one partner's death. p. 211

Random-type family or marriage: focuses on the needs of individuals and tends to value freedom, intensity, and spontaneity. p. 222

Rescue marriage: the couple base their relationship on the idea of healing. p. 221

Rite of passage: an event signaling a major change from one social status to another. p.207

Romantic marriage: a marriage filled with passion and sex. p. 221

Sexual exclusivity: each partner promises to have sexual relations only with the other. p.208

Static marriages: marriages that don't change over time, don't allow for changes in the spouses. p. 226

Total marriage: a marriage in which the partners are intensely bound together psychologically and participate in each other's lives in all areas and have few areas of tensions or conflict. p. 219

Traditional marriage: the husband is the income earner, and the wife takes care of the home and children. p. 221

Utilitarian marriage: a marriage based on convenience. p. 218

Vital marriage: a marriage in which the partners are intensely bound together psychologically and participate in each other's lives in many areas. p. 219

Vow renewal: a ceremony in which a couple repeat their commitment to each other. p. 227

Key People

Cuber, John, & Harroff, Peggy: writers of the book, *The Significant Americans*, and proposed that enduring marriages could be classified in five types.

Glick, Paul: coined the term "family life cycle" as describing families in stages of development.

Hochschild, Arlie: a sociologist who wrote the book, *The Second Shift*.

Kantor, David, & Lehr, William: writers of the book, *Inside the Family*, in which they suggested there are three types of family systems.

Wallerstein, Judith, & Blakeslee, Sandra: writers of the book, *The Good Marriage: How and Why Love Lasts*, in which they proposed four types of good marriages.

Practice Test

1. According to the text, Television today:
   A. portrays families that lack domestic perfection but provide warmth
   B. portrays families as pretentiously functional
   C. portrays families as weak and chaotic
   D. embraces weird and unrealistic families

2. The United States today has the _____ marriage rate among the advanced industrial countries.
   A. lowest
   B. highest
   C. most modest
   D. most variable

3. Studies show that adolescents and adults alike seem to have _____ expectations for the wedded state and are _____ for the realities of marriage and family life.
   A. low, eager
   B. modest, ready
   C. high, unprepared
   D. exaggerated, uneducated

4. Marriage has traditionally been defined as a socially approved mating relationship and:
   A. a legal union between a man and a woman
   B. a civil union between any two consenting adults
   C. a contractual relationship between males and females
   D. a civil convenience

5. David Knox suggests three positive reasons for marrying, they are all of the following EXCEPT:
   A. emotional security
   B. companionship
   C. desire to be a parent
   D. economic security

6. In a study of the never married, the majority said what they would miss most if they never did marry was:
   A. sex
   B. companionship
   C. emotional security
   D. having children

7. The average cost of a wedding in the United States in 2002 was:
   A. $10,400
   B. $ 3,200
   C. $21,300
   D. $32,200

8. Miscegenation:
   A. refers to the legal union between a man and a woman
   B. is marriage between a white person and a person of another race
   C. refers to the traits being passed from one generation to another
   D. is self-stimulation of the genitals for sexual pleasure

9. Rite of passage:
   A. is an event signaling a major change from one social status to another
   B. is a couple's way of signaling to the world they intend to marry
   C. is a socially sanctioned period that the couple may freely have sex
   D. is a period of time the couple use to recover from the stress of the wedding

10. In making a pledge of monogamous marriage, most partners assume their relationship will be built around:
    A. equality of labor
    B. economic stability
    C. sexual exclusivity
    D. tolerance and acceptance

11. A covenant marriage:
    A. is an agreement as to how property will be divided if divorce occurs
    B. is an antidivorce contract
    C. is a legal agreement worked out after the couple is married
    D. means each partner promises to have sexual relations only with the other

12. In a family life cycle, members' roles and relationships change:
    A. depending upon the economic status and success of the wage earners
    B. depending on the absence or presence of child-rearing responsibilities
    C. significantly when a geographical move is made
    D. based on the degree of function or dysfunction of the parents

13. Identity bargaining:
    A. means getting to know your partner's family members and friends
    B. occurs when you find yourself sorely frustrated by the confinements of marriage
    C. is adjusting your idealized expectations of your partner
    D. occurs when your partner suggests a prenuptial agreement

14. Generally, marital satisfaction is lowest:
     A. during the beginning phase of the family life cycle
     B. during the development of career and domestic roles
     C. during the child-rearing phase
     D. during the aging phase

15. Couples often experience the empty-nest syndrome, which is:
     A. when both sets of their parents have died
     B. when their adult children, being away awhile, now return
     C. a feeling of depression after the children move away
     D. when the last child enters grade school

16. A utilitarian marriage:
     A. is characterized by ongoing tension and unresolved conflict
     B. is based on convenience
     C. is one that thrives on conflict
     D. acknowledges incompatibility is pervasive & conflict always a potential

17. A passive-congenial marriage:
     A. is based on practicality, not emotion
     B. is fundamentally rewarding
     C. is one in which the partners have lost strong emotional connection
     D. is seen as a lost cause but the couple is resigned to it

18. A vital marriage is best characterized by the statement:
     A. We intensely enjoy being together & sharing every area of our lives
     B. We enjoy being together and sharing most of our lives
     C. We thrive on conflict
     D. Our marriage is based on practicality, not emotion

19. A companionate marriage is best characterized by the statement:
     A. We're making up for our past unhappiness
     B. He's the breadwinner, she's the homemaker
     C. We have a friendly, egalitarian relationship
     D. Our passion will last forever

20. A random-type family is best characterized by the statement:
     A. We value consent; both the family & the individual are important
     B. We value tradition; the family is most important
     C. We value freedom; the individual is most important
     D. We value economic success; the largest wage earner is most important

21. Heterogamous marriages:
    A. are between partners who have similar backgrounds
    B. have partners of different backgrounds and social characteristics
    C. are measured in terms of stability, happiness, and flexibility
    D. are between couples who base their relationship on equality and friendship

22. A study of 459 successfully married women found all of the following characteristics important EXCEPT:
    A. shared interests
    B. strong family ties on both sides
    C. similar views on children
    D. similar communication patterns

23. According to the text, the first thing to realize about marriage is that it is a:
    A. destination
    B. journey
    C. mindset
    D. major responsibility

24. According to the text, couples in happy marriages see their union as:
    A. a long-term commitment
    B. continuing so long as they both shall love
    C. a binding legal contract
    D. a long-term passionate, romantic relationship

25. A personal marriage agreement is:
    A. legally binding in most states
    B. a written agreement of how a married couple will behave
    C. a ceremony in which a couple repeat their commitment to each other
    D. usually not helpful in defining roles and expectations in the relationship

Project Suggestions

Project 1

If you were married and decided to have a personal marriage agreement, what specific items would you include? What would want in terms of division of labor, money management, sexual relations? Do you feel a personal marriage agreement would be helpful for you or not?

Project 2

When you look at the marriages of people you know, would you describe them as static or flexible? Was your parents' marriage static or flexible? How do you think the state of their marriage affected you? Describe.

Project 3

Go to the website *www.suite101.com/article.cfm/interfaith_relationships* and read the advice on interfaith relationships and marriages. What do you think? Do you agree or disagree?

Answer Key

1. A (p.201)	6. B (p.203)	11. B (p.209)	16. B (p.218)	21. B (p.223)
2. B (p.202)	7. C (p.203)	12. B (p.213)	17. A (p.219)	22. D (p.224)
3. C (p.202)	8. B (p.205)	13. C (p.213)	18. B (p.219)	23. B (p.226)
4. A (p.202)	9. A (p.207)	14. C (p.216)	19. C (p.221)	24. A (p.226)
5. D (p.203)	10. C (p.208)	15. C (p.216)	20. C (p.222)	25. B (p.227)

Chapter 8

VARIATIONS:

Nonmarital Families & Households

Learning Objectives

At the end of this chapter, you ought to be able to answer the following questions:

1. What kind of alternative household structure might I consider good for me?
2. What kind of single am I or could I be?
3. What is my understanding of homosexuality, and how does it relate to the research?
4. Would I ever consider communal living, group marriages, or open marriage?

Chapter Summary

8.1 Different Family & Household Relationships
  • Three new family structure variations are (1) platonic "roommate marriages," (2) commuter and transnational marriages, and (3) grandparents raising children alone.
  • In "roommate marriages" there is no sexual bond, but the roommates develop a deep emotional attachment for each other. In a commuter marriage each partner lives in a different location yet still committed to the family. Transnational marriages have one partner living in the U.S. and the other living in another country.
  • Skipped-generation households are family structures in which grandparents raise grandchildren.

8.2 The Single Way of Life
  • The single way of life includes the never-married, widowed, and divorced.
  • Trends toward the single life include the sex ratio, economic changes, and more liberal sexual and social standards.
  • The widowed represent approximately 7% of the adult population in the U.S.
  • The divorced are about 10% of the adult population in the U.S.
  • Nearly 4 million people ages 25–34 live with their parents, a trend driven by economic realities during recessionary times.
  • Among the stereotypes of singles are that singles are self-centered, financially better off, happier, and confirmed in their singlehood.

- Singles can be classified according to a typology of whether (1) they are voluntarily or involuntarily single and (2) their singlehood is temporary or stable.
- Singles can be classified according to five types: free-floating, open-couple, closed-couple, committed, and accommodationist.
- The median income for single mothers is significantly lower than the median income for two-parent households. Children of single parents tend to have higher incidences of drug use and psychiatric illness.

8.2   The Gay & Lesbian Way of Life
- Sexual orientation refers to sexual inclinations, such as one's feelings and sexual interactions, whether for the opposite gender, same gender, or both.
- Homosexuality is the sexual inclination toward members of the same gender. Bisexuality is the sexual inclination toward both genders.
- Accurate statistics regarding the percentage of gay men in the U.S. are difficult to obtain.
- Research on the acquisition of a gay identity looks at biological and environmental factors, with evidence supporting both views.
- Homoeroticism is erotic attraction to a member of the same gender.
- Homophobia, or antigay prejudice, is defined as negative attitudes toward homosexuality and homosexuals.
- Gay couples are more egalitarian in their dual-worker relationships than straight couples.
- Gay men seem to have more casual sex than either heterosexual men or lesbians, and their sexuality seems to be more body-centered than personality-centered.
- Domestic partners are two people, gay or straight, who have chosen to cohabit or share one another's lives in an intimate and committed relationship without being married. A civic union is a civil status similar to marriage, typically created for the purposes of allowing gay couples access to the benefits enjoyed by married heterosexuals.
- Many gays have children who were born when their fathers and mothers were part of a heterosexual marriage, before "coming out."

8.3   Communal Living, Group Marriages, & Open Marriages
- A commune is a group of adults, perhaps including children, who live together, sharing different aspects of their lives.
- Group marriages are marriages in which each member of the group is married to all other group members of the opposite sex.
- In an open marriage, the couple agree that each may have emotional and sexual relations with others. Open marriages may also involve swinging, in which couples exchange partners to engage in purely recreational sex.

Chapter Outline

- We give some examples of newer forms of living arrangements. We then discuss the world of singles and single parents. Next we discuss gay and lesbian relationships. We conclude with a discussion of communal relationships.

8.1   DIFFERENT FAMILY & HOUSEHOLD RELATIONSHIPS

Major Question: What kind of alternative household structure might I consider good for me?

    a.   Different Ways of Living: Three Examples
        i.   Platonic "Roommate Marriages"
            1.   People living as roommates for years with no sexual bond, but develop a deep emotional attachment to each other.
        ii.   Living Apart: Commuter & Transnational Marriages
            1.   A commuter marriage is a dual-career marriage in which each partner lives in a different geographical area, yet the pair still maintain their commitment to their family.
            2.   Transnational marriages are those in which one partner is in the U.S. and the other, perhaps with children, are in another country.
        iii.   Skipped-Generation Households: Grandparents Raising Grandchildren
            1.   Skipped-generation households are family structures in which grandparents raise grandchildren.
    b.   New Family Arrangements
        i.   Traditional Families, Nonfamily Households, & Alternative Arrangements
            1.   A traditional family is a unit made up of two or more people who are related by blood, marriage, or adoption and who live together.
            2.   A Nonfamily consists of (1) a person who lives alone or (2) people who live with unrelated individuals within a housing unit.
            3.   A lifestyle is the pattern by which a person organizes his or her living arrangements in relations to others.
        ii.   Principal Shifts In Household Arrangements
            1.   Between 1970 and 2000 U.S. households with married couples dropped from 70.6% to 52.5%.
            2.   Between 1970 and 2000 U.S. households with children dropped from 45.8% to 34%.
        iii.   The Reasons for Changes in Families & Households
            1.   Women's age at marriage and childbearing is increasing
            2.   Families and households have gotten smaller
            3.   More burden on working parents that support children and relatives

4. More female households
5. More women workers

8.2 THE SINGLE WAY OF LIFE

Major Question: What kind of single am I or could I be?

a. The World of Heterosexual Singles
    i. The Never-Married
        1. Never-married singles consist of those who would like to get married.
        2. Trends that encourage people to not marry include a lack of potential marriage partners due to the sex ratio.
        3. Economic changes may make marriage at earlier ages seem less attractive.
        4. Because of society's relatively greater tolerance of cohabitation, more people may be postponing or rejecting marriage.
    ii. The Widowed
        1. About 7% of the adult population in the U.S. consists of widows and widowers, down from 8% in 1980.
    iii. The Divorced
        1. About 10% of the adult population in the U.S. consists of single divorced men and women, up from 6.2% in 1980.

b. Myths & Realities about Singles
    i. What's Not True about Singles
        1. Singles are self-centered
        2. Singles are financially better off
        3. Singles are happier
        4. Singles are confirmed in their singlehood
    ii. What Is True about Singles
        1. Singles have more free time
        2. Singles have more fun
        3. Singles tend to be more comfortable with other singles
        4. Singles are lonely

c. Different Kinds of Singles
    i. Is Singlehood Voluntary or Involuntary, Temporary or Stable?
        1. Voluntary temporary singles are those who are open to marriage but find seeking a mate a lower priority than other activities.
        2. Voluntary stable singles are those who are satisfied not to be married.
        3. Involuntary temporary singles are those who would like to marry and are actively seeking mates.
        4. Involuntary stable singles are those who would like to marry, have not found a mate, and have come to accept their single status

ii.   Is Singlehood Freely Chosen?

1.   The free-floating single is an unattached single who dates randomly.

2.   The open-couple single has a steady partner, but the relationship is open enough that he or she can have romantic or sexual relationships with others.

3.   The closed-couple single is expected to be faithful to his or her partner.

4.   The committed single lives in the same household with his or her partner and has agreed to maintain fidelity to the relationship.

5.   The accommodationist single has accommodated herself or himself to an unattached life, getting together with friends but refusing romantic or sexual contacts.

iii.   Singlehood: Lifestyle Choice or Life Stage?

1.   Being single can be a lifestyle choice and/or a life stage, an interval between other arrangements.

d.   Being a Single Parent

i.   Single Mothers Raising Children

1.   The number of families in the U.S. headed by single mothers increased 25% from 1990 to 2000.

ii.   Single Fathers Raising Children

1.   Single-father households increased 62% in the U.S. during the decade of 1990 to 2000.

iii.   The Challenges to Single Parenting

1.   Money matters—the median income for an unmarried female head of household is $23,000, compared with $51,681 for two-parent households.

2.   Children's stability—children of single parents tend to have higher incidences of drug use and psychiatric illness.

8.3   THE GAY & LESBIAN WAY OF LIFE

Major Question: What is my understanding of homosexuality, and how does it relate to the research?

a.   Sexual Orientation: Heterosexuality, Homosexuality, & Bisexuality

i.   The Three Kinds of Sexual Orientation

1.   Heterosexuality: the sexual inclination toward members of the opposite gender

2.   Homosexuality: the sexual inclination toward members of the same gender

3.   Bisexuality: the sexual inclination toward both genders

ii.   Is One Out of Ten People Gay?

1.   Various studies report a range of 1% to 10% of their study sample were homosexual.

iii. The Problem of Trying to Determine the Percentage of Gays
1. The variety of study outcomes may be due to different study approaches, reluctance to reveal orientation, changing sexual behavior, sexual orientation not being expressed just through behavior, and sexual orientation may lie along a continuum.

b. Acquiring a Gay Identity
i. Sexual Identity: Chance or Choice?
1. Some studies indicate sexual orientation can be traced to genetics, yet other studies report people being able to change their sexual orientation.
ii. Four Stages of Acquiring a Gay or Lesbian Identity
1. Sensitization: "Am I different?"
2. Identity confusion: "I'll prove I'm not gay."
3. Identity assumption: "I know I'm gay, but which people should I tell?"
4. Commitment: "I'm gay, but that's not all I am."

c. Prejudice, Discrimination, & Violence against Gays
i. Anti-Gay Prejudice Can Escalate
1. Stage 1—offensive language
2. Stage 2—discrimination
3. Stage 3—violence
ii. The Roots of Anti-Gay Feelings
1. Personal insecurity
2. Fundamentalist religion
3. Ignorance about homosexuality

d. Gay Couples
i. Five Types of Gays: From "Happily Married" to Lonely
1. Closed couples—the "happily married"
2. Open couples—the "unhappily married"
3. The functionals—the highly sexual
4. The dysfunctionals—the tormented
5. The asexuals—the lonely
ii. How Gay Couples Differ from Straight Couples
1. More egalitarian, dual-worker relationships
2. Less family support and openness
iii. Gay Relationships
1. Gay men seem to have more casual sex than either heterosexual men or lesbians, and their sexuality seems to be more body-centered than personality-centered
2. Gay women seem to emphasize committed relationships more than gay men do, have less casual sex, and their sexuality is more personality-centered than body-centered

e.   Same-Sex Commitments
- i.   Six Stages in a Gay Relationship
  1. Year 1—blending: characterized by intense feelings, frequent sex
  2. Years 2–3—nesting: less sex, ambivalence, explore compatibility
  3. Years 4–5—maintaining: establish traditions, resolve conflicts
  4. Years 6–10—building: establish both independence and dependence
  5. Years 11–20—releasing: trust deepens, take each other for granted
  6. Years 20 on—renewing: feel secure, history of shared experiences
- ii.   Domestic Partners & Civil Unions
  1. Domestic partners are two people, gay or straight, who have chosen to cohabit in an intimate and committed relationship without being married.
  2. Civil unions are a status similar to marriage, created for the purposes of allowing gay couples access to the benefits enjoyed by married heterosexuals.
- iii.   Where Are Civil Unions Allowed?
  1. Canada, Denmark, Finland, Germany, Iceland, Norway, Sweden, Switzerland, Britain, Netherlands, and Belgium
  2. Within the U.S., the states of Vermont and Massachusetts

f.   Gays as Parents: The "Gayby Boom"
- i.   Having Children by Adoption
  1. Second-parent adoptions are situations in which the gay or lesbian partner of a biological or adoptive parent is given full legal status as the child's second parent.
  2. A foster parent is an adult who raises a child who is not his or her own for a short period of time but does not formally adopt that child.
- ii.   Having Children by Biological Means
  1. Gay men having children—using surrogate mothers
  2. Lesbians having children—using sperm donors

g.   How Are Children Affected by Having Gay Parents?
  1. Opponents worry that gays will push children into a gay lifestyle or engage in child molestation; gays say that such concerns are misplaced.

8.4   COMMUNAL LIVING, GROUP MARRIAGES, & OPEN MARRIAGES

Major Question: Would I ever consider communal living, group marriage, or open marriage?

- a. Communes
    - i. Types of Communal Living
        1. College living arrangements
        2. Elder living arrangements
        3. Co-housing communities
        4. Israeli farming cooperatives
- b. Group Marriages
    - i. In group marriages, each member of the group is married to all other group members of the opposite sex
- c. Open Marriages
    - i. In an open marriage, the couple agree that each may have emotional and sexual relations with others

Key Terms

Accommodationist single: one who has accommodated himself or herself to an unattached life, getting together with friends but refusing romantic or sexual contacts. p.245

Adoption: the legal process by which adult couples or singles voluntarily take a child born of other parents and raise him or her as their own child. p.260

Anti-gay prejudice: negative attitudes toward homosexuality and homosexuals. p.254

Artificial insemination: a process in which male semen is introduced artificially into the woman's vagina or uterus at about the time of ovulation. p.261

Bisexuality: the sexual inclinations toward both genders. p.249

Civil unions: a civil status similar to marriage, typically created for the purposes of allowing gay couples access to the benefits enjoyed by married heterosexuals. p.258

Closed-couple single: a person expected to be faithful to his or her partner. p.245 **"Come out":** when a homosexual publicly reveals his gayness. p.252

Committed single: one who lives in the same household with his or her partner and perhaps is engaged to be married or has agreed to maintain fidelity to the relationship. p.245

Commune: a group of adults, perhaps including children, who live together, sharing different aspects of their lives. p.265

Commuter marriage: a dual-career marriage in which each partner lives in a different geographical area, yet the pair still maintain their commitment to their family. p.236

Discrimination: an act of unfair treatment directed against an individual or group p.252

Domestic partners: two people, gay or straight, who have chosen to cohabit in an intimate and committed relationship without being married. p.258

Erotic feelings: feelings of sensuality or sexuality. p.251

Family: a unit made up of two or more people who are related by blood, marriage, or adoption and who live together. p.237

Foster parent: an adult who raises a child who is not his or her own for a short period of time but does not formally adopt that child. p.260

Free-floating single: an unattached single who dates randomly. p.245

Gay: refers to male homosexuals. p.249

Group marriage: each member of the group is married to all other group members of the opposite sex. p.266

Heterosexuality: the sexual inclination toward members of the opposite gender. p.248

Homoeroticism: when erotic attraction is directed toward a member of the same gender. p.251

Homophobia: negative attitudes toward homosexuality and homosexuals. p.254

Homosexuality: the sexual inclination toward members of the same gender. p.249

Involuntary stable singles: those who would like to marry, have not found a mate, and have come to accept their single status. p.244

Involuntary temporary singles: those who would like to marry and are actively seeking mates. p.244

Lesbian: refers to female homosexuals. p.249

Lifestyle: the pattern by which a person organizes his or her living arrangements in relations to others. p.238

Nonfamily household: a person who lives alone or people who live with unrelated individuals within a housing unit. p.237

Open marriage: a married couple agrees that each may have emotional and sexual relations with others while still keeping the marriage the primary relationship. p.267

Open-couple single: one who has a steady partner, but the relationship is open enough that he or she can have romantic or sexual relationships with others. p.245

Prejudice: an attitude of prejudging, usually negative, or an individual or group. p.252

Procreation: the bringing forth of children. p.248

Second-parent adoptions: situations in which the gay or lesbian partner of a biological or adoptive parent is given full legal status as the child's second parent. p.260

Sex ratio: the ratio of men to women within a particular social group. p.241

Sexual orientation: refers to sexual inclinations, feelings and sexual interactions, whether for the opposite gender, the same gender, or both. p. 248

Sexually open marriage: a married couple agrees that each may have emotional and sexual relations with others while still keeping the marriage the primary relationship. p.267

Single: among heterosexuals, the never-married, widowed, or divorced. p.241

Sperm bank: a depository for storing sperm. p.261

Sperm donor: a male who makes his sperm available for artificial insemination. p.261

Surrogate mother: a gay man might decide to adopt a baby through arrangements with a birth mother, known as a surrogate, who is artificially inseminated by a gay man. p.261

Swinging: an arrangement in which committed couples exchange partners to engage in purely recreational sex. p.267

Transnational marriages: marriages in which one partner is in the U.S. and the other, perhaps with children, is in another country. p.236

Voluntary stable singles: those who are satisfied not to be married. p.244

Voluntary temporary singles: those who are open to marriage but find seeking a mate a lower priority than other activities. p.244

Key People

Staples, Robert: writer and researcher that suggests singles can be classified according to five types based on whether or not their status is freely chosen.

Stein, Peter: writer and researcher that suggests that singles can be classified according to a typology of voluntary/involuntary and temporary or stable.

Troiden, Richard R.: created a model of the process of identifying oneself as gay occurring in four stages.

Practice Test

1. In platonic "roommate marriages":
    A. roommates develop deep emotional attachments to each other
    B. establish a very stable sexual bond
    C. are less common in urban areas with high housing costs
    D. are seldom a successful training ground for intimacy

2. About ____ of the adult population in the U.S. consists of single divorced men and women.
    A. 23%
    B. 7%
    C. 10%
    D. 27%

3. The number of households with three generations under one roof has ____ in the past 20 years.
    A. tripled
    B. doubled
    C. declined
    D. increased

4. A commuter marriage:
    A. is typically a single-career partnership
    B. is a dual career marriage with each partner in a different geographical area
    C. is a marriage with each partner having to travel to their work assignment
    D. is most successful when there are children present

5. U.S. families headed by single mothers increased ____ from 1990 to 2000.
    A. 25%
    B. 20%
    C. 15%
    D. 35%

6. Transnational marriages:
    A. are marriages between people of different nationalities
    B. are those with one partner in the U.S. and the other in another country
    C. are atypical of Latino immigrant marriages
    D. are typically experienced over very short periods of time

7. Skipped-generation households:
    A. are characterized by the absence of children
    B. consist of children living in grandparent-headed households
    C. are characterized by greater financial freedom
    D. are typically African-Americans between ages of 50 and 64

8. A traditional family:
    A. often includes foster families
    B. is a unit made up of people related by blood, marriage, or adoption
    C. in some states includes homosexual couples
    D. often consists of couples who cohabit

9. A "lifestyle" is:
    A. implies an absence of choice
    B. the pattern a person organizes his/her living arrangement with others
    C. not the same as alternative arrangements
    D. commonly associated with the traditional family concept

10. The median age at first marriage has been _____ since the 1950s.
    A. declining
    B. rising
    C. stationary
    D. statistically insignificant

11. During the first half of the 20th century, most people tended to marry, and to marry at younger ages. Since then, the trend has _____
    A. increased
    B. decreased
    C. reversed
    D. leveled off

12. Sociologist Peter Stein suggest more people are moving away from marriage and family norms as these norms conflict with the possibility for _____.
    A. economic advancement
    B. individual development
    C. sexual freedom
    D. advancing social status

13. Widowed females are less apt to find new spouses because _____.
    A. of the marriage gradient
    B. their tendency to be older
    C. they are less sexually desirable
    D. they tend to be economically disadvantaged

14. Presently, about _____ of the adult population in the U.S. consists of single divorced men and women.
    A. 21%
    B. 32%
    C. 3%
    D. 10%

15. According to the text, what is true about singles is:
    A.   singles are happier
    B.   singles are financially better off
    C.   singles are confirmed in their singlehood
    D.   singles have more fun

16. According to the text, what is NOT true about singles is:
    A.   singles have more free time
    B.   singles tend to be more comfortable with other singles
    C.   singles are lonely
    D.   singles are self-centered

17. Voluntary stable singles are:
    A.   those who are satisfied not to be married
    B.   those who are open to marriage
    C.   those who have not found a mate yet, and accept their single status
    D.   those who would like to marry and are actively seeking a mate

18. The accommodationist single:
    A.   is unattached and dates randomly
    B.   is expected to be faithful to his partner
    C.   has a steady partner but can have romance and sex with others
    D.   has adjusted himself or herself to an unattached life

19. Heterosexuality:
    A.   refers to sexual inclinations, feelings, and sexual interactions
    B.   sexual inclinations toward members of the opposite gender
    C.   sexual inclinations toward both genders
    D.   sexual inclinations toward members of the same gender

20. The problem of trying to determine the percentage of gays includes:
    A.   sexual orientation is not expressed just through behavior
    B.   consistent study approaches
    C.   quickness to reveal orientation
    D.   consistent sexual behavior

21. According to the text, biphobia is:
    A.   negative attitudes toward homosexuals
    B.   a mental dysfunction of two significant fears
    C.   negative attitudes toward bisexuality
    D.   exactly the same as anti-gay prejudice

22. In terms of the types of gay people, the dysfunctionals:
    A. report suffering many problems from their sexual orientation
    B. engage in a variety of sexual activity & construct their lives around sex
    C. tend to seek sexual satisfaction outside their relationship
    D. derive personal satisfaction from their partner and not others

23. In terms of characteristics of gay relationships, gay men:
    A. emphasize committed relationships
    B. have more casual sex than heterosexuals and lesbians
    C. are more personality-centered in their sexuality
    D. report less violence in their sexual relationships

24. Domestic partners:
    A. have a civil status similar to marriage
    B. are two people, gay or straight, who cohabit in a committed relationship
    C. are two gays who cohabit in a committed relationship
    D. are legally recognized in 37 states

25. A commune is:
    A. members of a group that are married to all other members of the group
    B. a group who exchange partners for recreational sex
    C. a group of people who live together sharing different aspects of life
    D. a married couple who agree each may have emotional relations with others

Project Suggestions

Project 1
Go to *www.unmarried.org* and explore the information on alternatives to marriage. What did you find the most interesting? Did you find anything you reacted to strongly? What was it? Why did you respond that way?

Project 2
What do you think, is it possible for you to have a loving relationship that is sexually or emotionally "open" or non-monogamous? Why?

Project 3
In terms of the debate on homosexuality being genetic or a choice, what do you believe? What do you base your opinion on? Studies? People you know? Religious beliefs? Write a paragraph on your position.

Answer Key

1. A (p.235)	6. B (p.236)	11. C (p.241)	16. D (p.243)	21. C (p.254)
2. C (p.235)	7. B (p.236)	12. B (p.242)	17. A (p.244)	22. A (p.256)
3. B (p.235)	8. B (p.237)	13. A (p.242)	18. D (p.245)	23. B (p.257)
4. B (p.235)	9. B (p.238)	14. D (p.242)	19. B (p.248)	24. B (p.258)
5. A (p.235)	10. B (p.239)	15. D (p.243)	20. A (p.250)	25. C (p.265)

Chapter 9 Communication:

Realizing Effective Intimacy

Learning Objectives

At the end of the chapter, you ought to be able to answer the following questions:
1.   What should I be aware of about how power works in a relationship
2.   What are principal areas of relationship conflict, how do people handle it, and how can I fight fair?
3.   How can I be better at communicating with my partner?

Chapter Summary

9.1   Power & Intimacy
- Power is the ability or potential to impose one's will on other people, to get them to think, feel, or do something they would not ordinarily have done spontaneously.
- Six different types of power in relationships are as follows: (1) Coercive power, (2) Reward power, (3) Expert power, (4) Legitimate power, (5) Referent power, (6) Informational power.
- The resource theory suggests that the balance of power in a marriage reflects the relative resources of each spouse.
- The principle of least interest states that whoever has the least interest in the relationship has the most power.
- Stepfamilies represent the blending of families and consequently result in complicated power relationships.

9.2   Conflict & Growth
- Conflict is the process of interaction that results when the behavior of one person interferes with the behavior of another.
- Conflict in relationships can be negative conflict. Some negative types of conflict are: (1) Repressed anger, (2) Passive-aggression, (3) Scapegoating, and (4) Gaslighting.
- Conflict can also be positive for relationships by helping to clarify differences and keeping small issues from becoming big ones.
- Research indicates nine common areas of disagreement among couples involving such issues as household tasks, money, sex, loyalty, power, nurturance, privacy, children, and differences in style.

- A major area of conflict is the division of household labor.
- Six major types of methods of conflict resolution are: (1) parallel, (2) competing, (3) avoiding, (4) accommodating, (5) compromising, and (6) collaborating.
- Five guidelines for handling conflict are: (1) attack problems, (2) focus on specific issues, (3) be sensitive about timing and place, (4) say what you mean, (5) let your partner know that you're listening.

9.3   The Nature of Communication
- Communication can be verbal and nonverbal.
- Research suggests that women communicate emotionally, while men tend to communicate cognitively.
- Satir identifies four barriers to communication: (1) Placaters, (2) Blamers, (3) Computers, and (4) Distractors.
- Gottman suggests there are five predictors of divorce: (1) Contempt, (2) Criticism, (3) Defensiveness, (4) Stonewalling, (5) Belligerence.
- Self-disclosure means telling another person deep personal information and feelings about yourself.
- Research suggests that to communicate effectively, you need to create an environment that gives communication high priority and values others' viewpoints; share power and hopes, be specific, honest, and kind; and tell your partner what you want in positive terms, ask for information, and listen well.

Chapter Outline

- We discuss how power works in intimate relationships and some explanations. We then consider conflict, both positive and negative, and how couples can learn to fight fair. Finally, we describe types of intimate communication, barriers to it, and ways in which partners can communicate more effectively.

9.1   **POWER & INTIMACY**
Major Question: What should I be aware of about how power works in a relationship?
   a.   Power & the Effects of Unequal Power
          i.   What is Power & Why Is it important?
                1.   Power is the ability or potential to impose one's will on other people.
                2.   People who feel powerless are apt to become depressed and susceptible to physical and emotional disorders.
          ii.   What Unequal Power Does to Relationships
                1.   It affects self-esteem.
                2.   It inhibits satisfaction, love, and sharing of feelings.
                3.   It encourages manipulation.

b. How Power Works: Some Possible Explanations
    i. Raven & Colleagues' Six Types of Power in a Relationship
        1. Coercive power—"I'm worried you'll punish me."
        2. Reward power—"I'm going along with you in hopes that you'll reward me."
        3. Expert power—"You're the boss in this area."
        4. Legitimate power—"I agreed earlier to comply when you ask."
        5. Referent power—"I admire the things you do, so I want to please you."
        6. Informational power—"You've convinced me of your viewpoint, so I'll do as you want."
    ii. Blood & Wolfe's Resource Theory: "Whoever Has the Most Resources Has the Most Power"
        1. Money: The bigger income earner usually has a bigger say in how the income is spent.
        2. Sex: Sex can be a balance-of-power resource, men with economic power yielding to women with sexual power.
    iii. Waller's Principle of Least Interest: "Whoever Has the Least Interests in the Relationship Has the Most Power"
        1. The person who gains the most from a relationship is the most dependent and hence the least powerful

9.2 CONFLICT & GROWTH

Major Question: What are principal areas of relationship conflict, how do people handle it, and how can I fight fairly?

a. Out of Intimacy, Conflict
    i. Negative Conflict: Bad for Relationships
        1. Types of negative conflict are: repressed anger, passive-aggression, scapegoating, and gaslighting
    ii. Positive Conflict: Good for Relationships
        1. Conflict helps to clarify differences.
        2. Conflict keeps small issues from becoming big ones.
        3. Conflict can improve relationships.
b. What Do Couples Have Disagreements About?
    i. Household Tasks: Conflicts about "the Second Shift"
        1. The second shift is defined as the housework and child care that employed women do after returning home from their jobs.
    ii. Money: The Power of the Purse
        1. Money matters generate conflict because money represents secrecy, power, and value systems.
    iii. Sex: What Is the Conflict Really About?
        1. Conflicts about sex—he wants to have sex, but she does not
        2. Conflicts about sex disguised as differences about other matters
        3. Conflicts about other matters disguised as differences about sex
    iv Loyalty: Trust & Fidelity
        1. Trust—believing that your partner is supportive and honest

2. Fidelity—faithfulness sexually and to the vows of marriage both partners swore to
 v Power: The Issue of Control
  1. Power and control are about which person gets to decide what to do.
 vi. Nurturance: Conflict over Who Takes Care of Whom
  1. If one partner feels that his or her emotional needs are not being taken care of, there is apt to be conflict.
 vii. Privacy: Conflict over Aloneness versus Interaction
  1. People have different needs in being alone and together.
 viii. Children: Coping with Offspring
  1. Children can be a source of great joy yet they require a lot of energy and attention.
 ix. Differences in Style: Variations in Preferences, Temperaments, & Tastes
  1. Conflict comes with spouses being different in styles of living and being.
 c. How People Handle Conflict
  i. Competing: "Conflict is War, and Only One Can Win?"
  ii. Parallel: "If We Ignore the Problem, Maybe it Will Go Away"
  iii. Avoiding: "Let's Do Anything to Keep the Peace"
  iv. Accommodating: "Let's Try to Find a Harmonious Solution"
  v. Compromising: "Let's Seek a Solution We Can Both Live With"
  vi. Collaborating: "Let's Really Work to Benefit Us Both"
 d. Resolving Conflict: Five Rules for Fighting Fair & Preserving Your Relationship
  i. Attack Problems, Not Your Partner, & Avoid Negativity
  ii. Focus on Specific Issues, Use "I Feel" Language, & Avoid Mixed Messages
  iii. Be Sensitive about Timing & Place
  iv. Say What You Mean, Don't Use or Manipulate, & Ask for What You Want
  v. Let Your Partner Know That You're Listening—Really Listening—& Work toward Resolution

9.3 THE NATURE OF COMMUNICATION

Major Question: How can I be better at communicating with my partner?
 a. Nonverbal Communication
  i. Some Types of Nonverbal Communication: Five Kinds
   1. Nonverbal cues include: (1) interpersonal space, (2) eye contact, (3) facial expressions, (4) body movements and gestures, and (5) touch
  ii. The Uses of Nonverbal Communication: Six Functions
   1. It can complement our words—"I mean what I'm saying."
   2. It can contradict our words—"I don't really mean what I'm saying."

3. It can accent our words—"This nonverbal sign means I'm emphasizing what I'm saying."
4. It can repeat our words—"I meant what I said, and this nonverbal sign tells you so again."
5. It can substitute for our words—"This sign means the same as if I'd spoken."
6. It can help to regulate our communication—"This sign means I agree, disagree, or need to interrupt."

b. Gender Differences
   i. Do Women Mainly Communicate Emotionally?
      1. For women life is intimacy—seeking closeness
      2. Women engage in "rapport talk"—talk is an end in itself
      3. What women talk about—leisure and men
      4. Women's speech is personal, concrete, and tentative
   ii. Do Men Mainly Communicate Cognitively?
      1. For men life is a contest—seeking status
      2. Men engage in "rapport talk"—talk is used to accomplish specific purposes
      3. What men talk about—leisure
      4. Men's speech is abstract, authoritative, and dominant
   iii. The "Female-Demand/Male-Withdraw" Pattern
      1. In troubled marriages the wife frequently gives negative verbal expression and the husband withdraws.
   iv. How Satisfied Are Couples with Their Communication?
      1. One study reported 62% of the wives stated they expressed their feelings more openly and freely than their husbands did.

c. Barriers to Communication
   i. Satir's Four Styles of Miscommunication
      1. Placating—"Whatever makes you happy, dear."
      2. Blaming—"It's not my fault."
      3. Computing—"One could be angry if one allowed it."
      4. Distracting—"Oh my, there's something else I must deal with."
   ii. Gottman's Horseman of the Apocalypse: Five Types of Destructive Interactions
      1. Contempt—expresses that your partner is inferior or undesirable
      2. Criticism—making disapproving judgments
      3. Defensiveness—defending yourself and not listening
      4. Stonewalling—refusing to listen, particularly to complaints
      5. Belligerence—being provocative & challenging your partner's power and authority
   iii. Hostility & Detachment as Destructive Behaviors
      1. Hostility—the primary predictor of marital dissatisfaction for wives was the husband's hostile responsiveness
      2. Withdrawal—the primary predictor of unhappiness for husbands was their wives withdrawal

Key Terms

Accommodating style of conflict: you are unassertive but cooperative; you take a passive stance. (p.288)

Avoiding style of conflict: you are unassertive and uncooperative, and are concerned with neither your interests nor the other's but mainly with avoiding confrontation. p.287

Belligerence: is being provocative and challenging your partner's power and authority. p.297

Blamers: are people who always try to put the responsibility for any problem on someone else. p.296

Coercive power: is based on fear that your partner will inflict punishment. p.276

Collaborating style of conflict: you have a great deal of concern about advancing your interests but also those of your partner. p.288

Competing style of conflict: you are assertive and uncooperative, viewing conflict as a war in which you force your way in order to win. p.287

Compromising style of conflict: you are only somewhat assertive, but you are cooperative. p.288

Computers: are people who always pretend to be reasonable and not reveal their feelings, because they find emotions threatening. p.296

Conflict taboo: considers conflict and anger wrong, the opposite of cooperation and love. p.281

Conflict: the process of interaction that results when the behavior of one person interferes with the behavior of another. p.280

Contempt: communication interactions that express that your partner is inferior or undesirable. p.296

Criticism: is making disapproving judgments or evaluations about your partner. p.297

Defensiveness: is not listening but rather defending yourself against a presumed attack. p.297

Distractors: are people who avoid disclosing relevant feelings, so they never discuss a problem but instead change the subject. p.296

Expert power: is based on your opinion that your partner has specialized knowledge. p.276

Female-demand/male-withdraw pattern: an ongoing cycle in which the wife frequently gives negative verbal expression and the husband withdraws. p.295

Folk concept of the family: emphasizes support, understanding, happiness, and warm holiday rituals. p.281

Gaslighting: is when one partner, perhaps using sarcasm, constantly criticizes or denies the other's definition of reality, diminishing the other's self-esteem. p.282

Gunnysacking: saving up, or putting into an imaginary sack, grievances until they spill over. p.281

Informational power: is persuasive power; you are persuaded by your partner that what he or she wants is in your best interest. p.277

Legitimate power: is based on your partner's having the right to ask you and your having the duty to comply. p.277

Leveling: consists of being specific, authentic, and transparent about how you feel, especially about matters in your relationship that create conflict or hurt. p.298

Nonverbal communication: consists of messages sent outside the written or spoken word. p.291

Parallel style of conflict: you are unassertive and uncooperative, you and your partner completely deny and retreat from any discussion of a problem. p.287

Passive-aggression: is the expression of anger indirectly rather than directly. p.281

Placaters: are passive people who are always agreeable but act helpless. p.296

Power: the ability or potential to impose one's will on other people—to get them to think, feel, or do something they would not ordinarily have done spontaneously. p.275

Rapport talk: female communication style aimed primarily at gaining rapport or intimacy and is an end in itself. p.294

Referent power: is based on your identifying with and admiring your spouse and receiving satisfaction by pleasing him or her. p.277

Report talk: male communication style aimed primarily at conveying information and to accomplish specific purposes. p.294

Repressed anger: is the unconscious suppression of feelings of anger so that they are expressed in other ways. p.281

Resource theory: suggests that the balance of power in a marriage reflects the relative resources of each spouse. p.277

Reward power: is based on your belief that your agreement with your partner will elicit rewards from that partner. p.276

Scapegoating: is the blaming of one particular family member for nearly everything that goes wrong in that family. p.281

Second shift: is defined as the housework and child care that employed women do after returning home from their jobs. p.283

Self-disclosure: means telling another person deep personal information and feelings about yourself. p.297

Silent treatment: you either ignore your partner or verbally say that things are all right while sending nonverbal signals that they are not. p.281

Stonewalling: is refusing to listen to your partner, particularly his or her complaints. p.297

Key People

Blood, Robert, & Wolfe, Donald: sociologists who formulated the Resource Theory: "Whoever has the most resources has the most power."

Gottman, John: social psychologist and a leading authority on marital communication.

Hochschild, Arlie: sociologist who coined the term, second shift, defined as the housework and child care that employed women do after returning home from their jobs.

Malandro, Loretta, & Barker, Larry: authors of the book, *Nonverbal Communications*.

Raven, Bertram: writer and researcher who suggests there are six types of power in a relationship: coercive, reward, expert, legitimate, referent, and informational.

Satir, Virginia: author of two classic books on marital communication, *Peoplemaking* and *The New Peoplemaking*.

Tannen, Deborah: psychologist author of books about gender communication, such as *You Just Don't Understand*.

Waller, Willard: sociologist who formulated the Principle of Least Interest: "Whoever has the least interest in the relationship has the most power."

Practice Test

1. According to Dr. Raymond Friedman an important difference between email and conversation is:
    A. increased social cues
    B. reduced attention
    C. low feedback
    D. limited email length

2. According to the text, what has been the most common source of conflict for couples:
    A. sex
    B. money
    C. children
    D. relatives

3. According to the text, when does affection most cause resentment?
    A. women resent partners who are affectionate only when they want sex
    B. men resent partners who are affectionate only when they want to buy something
    C. parents resent affection when children try to manipulate them
    D. children resent affection when they feel they are being controlled

4. In _____ of divorces one or both partners had been sexually involved with someone outside the marriage.
    A. one-half
    B. one-fourth
    C. one-third
    D. three-quarters

5. Couples in lasting marriages show _____ times more positive feeling and interaction between them than negative.
    A. three
    B. two
    C. five
    D. seven

6. In intimate relationships, power inequality is important because:
    A. in inhibits satisfaction, love, and sharing of feelings
    B. it discourages manipulation
    C. it tends to have no effect upon a person's sense of self-esteem
    D. it enhances satisfaction, love, and sharing of feelings

7. Expert power is best characterized by the statement:
   A. "I'm worried you'll punish me"
   B. "You're the boss in this area"
   C. "I'm going along with you in hopes that you'll reward me"
   D. "I mean what I am saying"

8. Referent power is best characterized by the statement:
   A. "I admire the things you do, so I want to please you"
   B. "I agreed earlier to comply when you ask"
   C. "You've convinced me of your viewpoint, so I'll do as you want"
   D. "Whatever makes you happy, dear"

9. The Principle of Least Interest: "Whoever Has the Least Interest in the Relationship Has the Most Power" was coined by:
   A. Robert Blood
   B. Donald Wolfe
   C. Willard Waller
   D. Raymond Friedman

10. Passive-aggression is:
    A. the blaming of one particular family member for everything
    B. unconscious suppression of feelings of anger
    C. constantly criticizing other's definition of reality
    D. the expression of anger indirectly rather than directly

11. "When one partner, perhaps using sarcasm, constantly criticizes or denies the other's definition of reality, diminishing the other's self-esteem." This is a definition for:
    A. scapegoating
    B. repressed anger
    C. conflict taboo
    D. gaslighting

12. According to one study, how often do the majority of couples fight?
    A. every couple of days
    B. once a week
    C. one to two times a month
    D. once every two months

13. What is the primary area of conflict for most couples over time?
    A. power
    B. privacy
    C. household tasks
    D. children

14. Collaborating is best characterized by the statement:
    A. "Let's seek a solution we can both live with"
    B. "Let's try to find a harmonious solution"
    C. "Let's really work to benefit us both"
    D. "Let's do anything to keep the peace"

15. The style of conflict statement "Conflict is war, and only one can win" best describes the:
    A. parallel style
    B. competing style
    C. avoiding style
    D. accommodating style

16. According to the text, conflict is inevitable and the best way to deal with conflict:
    A. is staying silent
    B. is ignoring the problem
    C. is shouting and arguing
    D. is learning how to fight fair

17. The behavior of signaling the start and end of a conversation, expressing emotion, and signifying interest and attention, are characteristics of the nonverbal communication of:
    A. facial expression
    B. body movements and gestures
    C. touch
    D. eye contact

18. The author of the book on communication differences between men and women entitled, *Men Are from Mars, and Women Are from Venus*, is:
    A. Deborah Tannen
    B. John Gray
    C. Virginia Satir
    D. John Gottman

19. If any generalizations can be made about women, it is that when there are relationship problems, women approach them:
    A. cognitively
    B. emotionally
    C. rationally
    D. illogically

20. According to Deborah Tannen, women engage in "rapport talk," which is:
    A. aimed primarily at conveying information
    B. aimed primarily at gaining intimacy
    C. aimed primarily at feeling safe
    D. aimed primarily at the need to be understood

21. According to Deborah Tannen, generally, for men, life is:
    A. intimacy
    B. a contest
    C. all about sex
    D. about seeking power

22. The author of two classic books on marital communication, *Peoplemaking*, and *The New Peoplemaking*, is:
    A. Deborah Tannen
    B. John Gray
    C. Virginia Satir
    D. John Gottman

23. "Computing" is a style of miscommunication and is best characterized by the statement:
    A. "Oh my, there's something else I must deal with"
    B. "It's not my fault"
    C. "One could get angry if one allowed it"
    D. "Whatever makes you happy, dear"

24. In John Gottman's types of destructive interactions, "belligerence" is best characterized by the statement:
    A. "Look, I know what you're going to say, and I resent it"
    B. "Hey, you know barbequing is not your talent. Why bother?"
    C. "Just a minute, who elected you God?"
    D. "We've been over this before, and there's no point discussing it again"

25. In terms of communicating self-disclosure, the term "leveling" means:
    A. telling another person deep personal information about yourself
    B. being specific, authentic, and transparent about how you feel
    C. being honest and willing to recognize unpleasant things about yourself
    D. standing directly in front of a person and looking them in the eyes

Project Suggestions

Project 1
So, how well do you know your partner? Go to *www.gottman.com*, click on Marriage & Couples. Click on Relationship Quiz. Take the quiz. What did you find out about you and your partner? What surprised you?

Project 2
Experiment with affirming someone you have a friendship with. How do they respond to your affirming words? What does it feel like to affirm someone?

Project 3
The text says that for women, life is intimacy, and for men, life is a contest. Do you agree or disagree? Can you think of examples to illustrate your point of view?

Answer Key

1. C (p.273)	6. A (p.275)	11. D (p.282)	16. D (p.288)	21. B (p.294)
2. B (p.275)	7. C (p.276)	12. C (p.282)	17. D (p.292)	22. C (p.296)
3. A (p.275)	8. A (p.277)	13. C (p.283)	18. B (p.294)	23. C (p.296)
4. C (p.275)	9. C (p.279)	14. C (p.288)	19. B (p.294)	24. C (p.297)
5. C (p.275)	10. D (p.281)	15. B (p.287)	20. B (p.294)	25. B (p.298)

Chapter 10 REPRODUCTION:

Decisions about Having or Not Having Children

Learning Objectives

At the end of the chapter, you ought to be able to answer the following questions:

1. What are my feelings about having children, and what influences these feelings?
2. Which kind of birth control method would probably be best for me and my partner?
3. What have I learned about abortion and safe haven laws that I didn't know?
4. If I wanted children but had difficulty conceiving them, what would my options be?

Chapter Summary

10.1 Having or Not Having Children: Choice or Fate?

- There are four kinds of reactions partners have to pregnancy: (1) planner partners, (2) acceptance-of-fate partners, (3) ambivalent partners, (4) yes-no partners.
- Couples can choose: no children, having children later, having one child, or having several children.
- Child-free marriages involve a choice on the couple's part not to have children, yet they must deal with the cultural attitude that takes having children for granted.
- Couples might postpone having children to finish their education, establish their career, develop their relationship with each other, or to build the economic resources to provide for children.
- Social and economic factors influence people's decision to have children: (1) family size; (2) race, ethnicity, and religion; and (3) education, income, and workforce status.
- Fertility refers to both the ability to reproduce biologically and a person's actual reproductive performance.
- Fertility rates refer to the number of birth per year per thousand women of child-bearing age (ages 15–44).
- Raising children can be expensive.

10.2 Contraception
- Methods of birth control include: (1) natural family planning methods, (2) barrier methods, (3) hormonal methods, (4) sterilization, and (5) emergency contraception.
- Pregnancy "protection" approaches that often don't work include (1) no method at all, (2) breastfeeding, and (3) douching.
- Natural family planning methods of birth control include the calendar method, the BBT method, the cervical mucus method, and withdrawal.
- Periodic abstinence is avoidance of sexual intercourse during perceived fertile periods of the woman's menstrual cycle.
- The birth-control technique known as withdrawal, or coitus interruptus, consists of removing the penis from the vagina before ejaculation.
- Barrier methods of contraception involve the use of devices that put physical barriers between egg and sperm. They include diaphragms, cervical caps, and condoms.
- A diaphragm is a soft latex rubber dome stretched over a metal spring or ring.
- A cervical cap operates in much the same way as the diaphragm. It is a much smaller, thimble-shaped rubber or plastic cap that fits directly onto the cervix.
- The female condom is a lubricated, polyurethane pouch about 7 inches long that is inserted into the vagina and extends outside it to cover the outer lips.
- Hormonal methods are female forms of birth control that use chemicals to prevent ovulation.
- Oral contraceptives, The Pill, consist of synthetic female hormones that prevent ovulation or implantation.
- The vaginal ring is placed inside the vagina to go around the cervix; it releases the hormones progestin and estrogen.
- The intrauterine device (IUD) is a small, T-shaped plastic device that is inserted inside the uterus.
- Hormone injections are another form of contraception.
- Contraceptive hormones can also be implanted surgically.
- Sterilization is the surgical or nonsurgical interruption of a person's reproductive capacity.
- Male sterilization is accomplished by vasectomy.
- Female sterilization may be accomplished by removal of the ovaries or uterus.
- The Essure procedure is a form of female nonsurgical sterilization.
- Emergency contraception refers to various methods of protecting a woman from getting pregnant after having unprotected vaginal intercourse.

10.3 Abortion & Abandonment
- Abortion is the removal or expulsion of an embryo or fetus from the uterus before it can survive on its own.
- An abortion can happen spontaneously, owing to medical, hormonal, genetic, or other problems; this is called a spontaneous abortion, or miscarriage.
- Induced, or elective, abortion involves a decision to purposely terminate a pregnancy.

- Alternatives to abortion include deciding to keep the child, adoption, and foster care.
- If a pregnancy is unintended women who have an abortion seem not to experience negative psychological responses (1) if the idea of abortion does not violate their deeply held beliefs an (2) if it does not have a perceived social stigma.
- Safe haven laws allow a person, anonymously to leave an unwanted newborn at a hospital, fire station, or other designated place.

10.4   Infertility, Reproductive Technology, & Adoption
- Infertility is the failure to conceive after 1 year of regular sexual intercourse without contraception or the inability to carry a pregnancy to live birth. Infertility is differentiated from sterility, the total inability to conceive.
- Infertility may be caused by not enough sex, too much sex, sex at wrong times of the month, use of vaginal lubricants, anemia, fatigue, emotional stress, poor nutrition, and effects of STDs.
- Male infertility may be caused by low sperm count, blockage so that sperm can not pass from the testicle to the end of the penis, or erection or ejaculation problems.
- Infertility in females may be caused by age, failure to ovulate, blockage of the fallopian tubes, abnormalities of the uterus, or an inhospitable environment for sperm.
- Endometriosis is when cells from the inner lining of the uterus grow in the pelvic and abdominal cavities.
- Assisted reproductive technology is the name for all treatments and procedures by which human eggs and sperm may be manipulated to produce a pregnancy.
- In artificial insemination, sperm are collected from the male donor by masturbation.
- Fertility-enhancing drugs stimulate hormones to produce eggs.
- Through the in vitro fertilization procedure the fertilized egg is implanted in the wall of the uterus.
- In gamete intrafallopian transfer the egg and sperm are united inside the woman's fallopian tubes.
- In Zygote intrafallopian transfer a fertilized egg, or zygote, is placed in the woman's fallopian tubes.
- In embryo transfer, the male sperm is put in a woman's uterus during ovulation. Five days later, the embryo is transferred to the uterus of the male's infertile female partner, who carries the baby to birth.
- A surrogate mother is a consenting woman who is artificially inseminated with the sperm of the male partner of a woman who is infertile.
- Adoption is when a couple voluntarily takes a child of other parents and raises him or her as their own child.
- Public adoptions are arranged through licensed agencies that place children in adoptive families.
- Private adoptions are arranged directly between the birth mother and the adoptive parents.

- Closed adoptions are those in which birth parents and adoptive parents do not know one another's identities and don't communicate.
- Semi-open adoptions are those in which the biological parents and the adoptive parents exchange some information but don't otherwise communicate.
- Open adoptions are those in which birth parents and adoptive parents have active contact.
- Traditionally, people wanting to adopt have been couples who are infertile, are highly educated, have high incomes, or have wives not working full-time, or all of these.

Chapter Outline

- We discuss possible reactions to having children, the choices prospective parents have, what influences people to have children, and the costs of raising children. We then discuss five general methods of birth control. We next discuss abortion and safe haven laws. Finally, we describe causes of infertility, six types of assisted reproduction technology, and the subject of adoption.

10.1   HAVING OR NOT HAVING CHILDREN: CHOICE OR FATE?
Major Question: What are my feelings about having children, and what influences these feelings?

a.   How Would You React If You Suddenly Learned That You'll Be a Parent? Four reactions:
  i.   Planner Partners: "A Baby! Hallelujah!"
  ii.   Acceptance-of-Fate Partners: "What a Pleasant Surprise!"
  iii.   Ambivalent Partners: "We Really Didn't Want a Baby, but We'll Go Ahead with It"
  iv.   Yes-No Partners: "I Want a Baby, My Partner Doesn't, but I'll Have It Anyway."

b.   The Choices: Child-Free, Postponing Children, One Child, or Many Children?
  i.   Child-Free: Voluntarily Having No Children
    1.   Among American women ages 15–44, 8.9% have said that they don't expect to have children.
  ii.   Postponing Children: Having Babies Later
    1.   In 1998, 23% of American women had first babies at age 30.
  iii.   One Child: Are "Only Children" Different? Yes, In Positive Ways
    1.   In 2002, 29% of American couples only one child.
  iv.   More Than One Child
    1.   In 2000, 20% of American couples had two children.

c.   What Influences People to Have Children?
  i.   General Trends in Family Size
    1.   In general, families have been getting smaller, commonly just two children.

ii.　Race, Ethnicity, & Religion
　　　　　1.　Fertility rates vary for different ethnic and racial groups, with Hispanics having the highest rates and whites having the lowest. Catholics and Mormons tend to have higher fertility rates.
　　　iii.　Education, Income, & Workforce Status
　　　　　1.　Generally, the more education and income a woman has, the lower the fertility rate. Women not in the workforce tend to have the highest fertility rates.
　d.　The Costs of Raising Children
　　　i.　A middle-income family (earning $39,700–$66,900 a year) with two children might well spend 40—45% or more of their after-tax income on their offspring.

10.2 CONTRACEPTION: PRACTICAL METHODS OF BIRTH CONTROL

Major Question: Which kind of birth-control method would probably be best for me and my partner?

　a.　Contraceptive Choices
　　　i.　"Contraceptive" Methods That Usually Don't Work
　　　　　1.　No method at all: Using no method of contraception at all has the highest failure rate for birth control.
　　　　　2.　Breastfeeding: Nursing delays fertility, yet, it is an unreliable form of birth control.
　　　　　3.　Douching: Douching is the practice of rinsing out the vagina with a chemical solution right after sexual intercourse.
　　　ii.　Five Categories of Contraception
　　　　　1.　Natural family planning methods: abstinence, rhythm method, and withdrawal.
　　　　　2.　Barrier methods: condoms, diaphragms, and cervical caps.
　　　　　3.　Hormonal methods: pills, vaginal rings, insertion devices, skin patches, injections, or implants.
　　　　　4.　Sterilization: vasectomies for men, ligations for women.
　　　　　5.　Emergency contraception: morning-after pill, abortion pill.
　　　iii.　Natural Family Planning Methods: Periodic Abstinence & Withdrawal
　　　　　1.　Periodic abstinence is avoidance of sexual intercourse during perceived fertile periods of the woman's menstrual cycle.
　　　　　2.　Withdrawal consists of removing the penis from the vagina before ejaculation.
　　　iv.　Barrier Methods: Diaphragms, Cervical Caps, & Condoms Used with Spermicide
　　　　　1.　Diaphragm: a soft latex rubber dome stretched over a metal spring or ring.
　　　　　2.　Cervical cap: a thimble-shaped rubber or plastic cap that

fits directly onto the cervix.
- v. Hormonal Methods: Pill, Vaginal Ring, Insertion, Patch, Injection, & Implant
  1. Oral contraceptives: consist of synthetic female hormones that are administered in pill form and that prevent ovulation or implantation.
  2. Vaginal ring: a hormonal ring that is placed inside the vagina to go around the cervix; it releases the hormones progestin and estrogen.
  3. Insertion: the intrauterine device is a small, T-shaped plastic device that is inserted by a health-care professional inside the uterus.
  4. Hormone injection: contraception is available as hormone injection, requiring visits to a health-care provider.
  5. Implant: sticklike rods are implanted under the skin and release a low, steady level of a steroid that prevents pregnancy.
- vi. Sterilization: Surgical & Nonsurgical Methods
  1. Male surgical sterilization, vasectomy, involves making a pair of incisions in the scrotum, cutting and tying two sperm-carrying tubes.
  2. Female surgical sterilization, tubal ligation, involves the blocking or cutting of the fallopian tubes.
  3. Female nonsurgical sterilization, Essure, a tiny metal implant is put into the fallopian tube, the implant expands, and scar tissue grows around it, blocking the tube.
- vii. Emergency Contraception
  1. Morning-after pill, are combined estrogen-progesterone oral contraceptives, taken 72 hours within unprotected intercourse.
  2. RU-486: a synthetic steroid that prevents the uterine lining from getting the progesterone it needs to support a fertilized egg.

10.3 ABORTION & ABANDONMENT

Major Question: What have I learned about abortion and safe haven laws that I didn't know?

- a. Abortions: Spontaneous versus Induced
  - i. Spontaneous abortion: a miscarriage that occurs within the first 20 weeks of pregnancy.
  - ii. Induced abortion: a decision has been made to purposefully terminate a pregnancy.
- b. Abortion, Psychological Health, & Moral Issues
  - i. Psychological health: some women who lose their wanted babies become distraught and grieve, others feel little effect.
  - ii. Moral issues: abortion is an issue about which many Americans

profoundly disagree.
c. Safe Havens for Placing Abandoned Babies
    i. Safe haven laws allows a person—anonymously and without fear of prosecution—to leave an unwanted newborn at a hospital emergency room, fire station, or other designed place.

10.4 INFERTILITY, REPRODUCTIVE TECHNOLOGY, & ADOPTION

Major Question: If I wanted children but had difficulty conceiving them, what would my options be?

a. The Causes of Infertility
    i. The Causes of Infertility in Couples
        1. (1) not enough sex, (2) too much sex, (3) sex at wrong times of the month, (4) use of vaginal lubricants, (5) health problems
    ii. The Causes of Infertility in Males
        1. (1) low-quality sperm, (2) blockage, (3) erection or ejaculation problems
    iii. The Causes of Infertility in Females
        1. (1) age, (2) failure to ovulate, (3) blockage, (4) abnormalities of the uterus, (5) inhospitable environment for sperm

b. Treating Infertility: Assisted Reproductive Technology
    i. Artificial Insemination: AIH & AID
        1. AIH: artificial insemination by husband
        2. AID: artificial insemination by donor
    ii. Fertility-Enhancing Drugs: Ovulating-Stimulating Hormones
    iii. In Vitro Fertilization: "Test-Tube Babies"
        1. In Vitro Fertilization: the egg and sperm are taken from the parents and kept until the mother's uterus is hormonally ready, then the fertilized egg is implanted in the wall of the uterus.
    iv. Intrafallopian Transfer: GIFT & ZIFT
        1. GIFT: gamete intrafallopian transfer, the egg and sperm are collected, then united inside the fallopian tubes.
        2. ZIFT: zygote intrafallopian transfer, the egg and sperm are collected, 1 day after fertilization, the zygote is placed in the fallopian tubes.
    v. Embryo Transfer
        1. The sperm is placed in a fertile woman's uterus during ovulation. Five days later the embryo is moved to the uterus of the infertile woman.
    vi. Surrogate Mothers
        1. A surrogate mother is a consenting woman who is artificially inseminated with the sperm of the male partner of an infertile woman.

              vii.   When Fertility Treatment Fails
                     1.   The couple have to re-envision their life without a child.
    c.   Adoption
              i.   Public versus Private Adoptions
                     1.   Public adoptions are arranged by licensed agencies.
                     2.   Private adoptions are arranged directly between the birth mother and adoptive parents.
              ii.   Closed, Semi-open, or Open Adoptions
                     1.   Closed: those in which birth parents and adoptive parents do not know one another's identities and don't communicate.
                     2.   Semi-open: those in which the biological and adoptive parents exchange information such as photos or letters but don't otherwise communicate.
                     3.   Open: those in which both parents and adoptive parents have more active contact.
             iii.   Who Adopts?
                     1.   Traditionally, people wanting to adopt have been couples who are infertile, highly educated, high incomes, with wives not working full-time.
             iv.   Who Is Adopted?
                     1.   Most in demand are healthy white infants; hardest to place are older non-white children with physical and emotional disabilities.

Key Terms

Abortion: the removal or expulsion of an embryo or fetus from the uterus before it can survive on its own. p.327

Adoption: voluntarily taking the child of other parents as one's own child. p.337

Artificial insemination: sperm are collected by masturbation from a husband or donor and injected by syringe directly into the woman's vagina or uterus. p. 334

Assisted reproductive technology (ART): is the collective name for all treatments and procedures by which human eggs and sperm may be manipulated to produce a pregnancy. p.334

Barrier methods of contraception: devices that put physical barriers between egg and sperm: diaphragms, cervical caps, and condoms. p.319

Cervical cap: a small, thimble-shaped rubber or plastic cap that fits directly onto the cervix. p.319

Child-free marriage: a marriage that is voluntarily without children. p.308

Closed adoption: an adoption in which birth parents and adoptive parents do not know one another's identities and don't communicate. p.338

Colpotomy: an incision is made through the back of the vagina and closes the fallopian tubes. p.324

Combination pill: contains two hormones: estrogen and progestin.

Copper-T IUD: contains copper, which interferes with fertilization and implantation. p.322

Depo-Provera: a synthetic compound similar to progesterone that is injected into a woman's arm or buttock. p.322

Diaphragm: a soft latex rubber dome stretched over a metal spring or ring that covers the ceiling of the vagina, including the cervix. p.319

Douching: the practice of rinsing out the vagina with a chemical solution right after sexual intercourse. p.316

Down syndrome: a condition that leads to various degrees of mental retardation and physical disability. p.309

Embryo transfer: the sperm of a male partner of an infertile woman is placed in another woman's uterus during ovulation. Five days later, the embryo is transferred to the uterus of the infertile woman. p.336

Emergency contraception: or postcoital birth control, refers to various methods of protecting a woman from getting pregnant after having unprotected vaginal intercourse. p.325

Endometriosis: some cells of the inner lining of the uterus grow in the pelvic and abdominal cavities. p.333

Essure procedure: consists of a physician's inserting a tiny metal implant into the fallopian tubes using a thin tube that passes through the vagina and uterus. Once the tube is removed, the implant expands, and scar tissue grows around it, completely blocking the tube. p.325

Fertility rates: refer to the number of births per year per thousand women of child-bearing age (ages 15–44). p.312

Fertility: refers to both the ability to reproduce biologically and a person's actual reproductive performance. p.312

Fertility-enhancing drugs: drugs that stimulate hormones to produce eggs. p.334

GIFT, gamete intrafallopian transfer: the egg and sperm are collected and then united inside the woman's fallopian tubes. p.335

Hormonal methods: female forms of birth control that use chemicals to prevent ovulation or implantation of the fertilized egg in the uterus, using pills, vaginal rings, vaginal insertion, skin patches, injections, or implants. p.321

In vitro fertilization (IVF) procedure: the egg and sperm are taken from the parents and kept in a lab until the mother's uterus is hormonally ready; then the fertilized egg is implanted in the wall of the uterus. p.335

Induced abortion, or elective abortion: a decision has been made to purposefully terminate a pregnancy. p.327

Infertility: means the failure to conceive after 1 year of regular sexual intercourse without contraception or the inability to carry a pregnancy to live birth. p.332

Intrauterine device (IUD): a small, T-shaped plastic device inserted by a health-care professional inside the uterus. p.322

Intrauterine system: a small T-shaped device placed inside the uterus by a physician. It releases a small amount of hormone each day to prevent pregnancy. p.322

Laparoscopy: a tubelike instrument called a laparoscope is inserted through a half-inch incision in the area of the navel and closes the fallopian tubes. p.324

Laparotomy: a surgeon makes a 2-inch-long incision in the woman's abdomen and cuts the fallopian tubes. p.324

Lunelle: hormone shot given monthly in the arm, buttocks, or thigh. p.323

Mini-pill: contains only one hormone: progestin. p.321

Morning-after pill: a combined estrogen-progesterone oral contraceptive. p.325

Natural family planning methods of birth control: include (a) various ways of gauging times for periodic abstinence—the calendar method, the BBT method, the cervical mucus method—and (b) withdrawal. p.316

Nonoxynol-9: an antiviral, antibacterial spermicidal agent. p.315

Norplant: consists of small, removable silicone-rubber; sticklike rods that are implanted surgically by a physician, under a woman's skin. The rods release a low, steady level of steroid that prevents pregnancy. p.323

Open adoptions: those in which both birth parents and adoptive parents have more active contact and lifelong communication. p.338

Opportunity costs: the loss of wages and investments that parents sacrifice by devoting their time and energy to child rearing. p.313

Oral contraceptive, The Pill: consist of synthetic female hormones that are administered in pill form and that prevent ovulation or implantation. p.321

Periodic abstinence: or fertility awareness, natural family planning, rhythm method; is avoidance of sexual intercourse during perceived fertile periods of the woman's menstrual cycle. p.316

Private adoptions: adoptions arranged directly between birth mother and adoptive parents. p.337

Progestasert IUD: a small, plastic T-shaped device that contains the hormone progesterone. p.322

Pronatalist bias: the cultural attitude that takes having children for granted. p.309

Public adoption: adoptions arranged through licensed agencies. p.337

RU-486, or mifepristone: a synthetic steroid often referred to as the abortion pill. p.325

Safe haven laws, or abandoned-baby laws: allows a person—anonymously and without fear of prosecution—to leave an unwanted newborn at a hospital, fire station, or other designated place. p.331

Semi-open adoptions: those in which the biological and adoptive parents exchange information such as photos or letters but don't otherwise communicate. p.338

Spermicide: a sperm-killing chemical. p.319

Spontaneous abortion or miscarriage: an abortion that happens spontaneously owing to medical, hormonal, genetic, or other problems. p.327

Sterilization: the surgical or nonsurgical interruption of a person's reproductive capacity, generally for people who want a permanent method of birth control. p.323

Surrogate mother: a consenting woman who is artificially inseminated with the sperm of the male partner of a woman who is infertile. p.336

Tubal ligation or "tying the tubes": involves the blocking or cutting of the fallopian tubes to prevent passage of the eggs down to the uterus, where they might be fertilized. p.323

Vaginal ring: a hormonal ring that is placed inside the vagina to go around the cervix; it releases the hormones progestin and estrogen. p.321

Vasectomy: a surgical procedure that involves making a pair of incisions in the scrotum and cutting and tying two sperm-carrying tubes. p.323

Withdrawal, or coitus interruptus: consists of removing the penis from the vagina before ejaculation. p. 319

ZIFT, zygote intrafallopian transfer: the egg and sperm are collected and placed in a lab dish. One day after fertilization takes place, the zygote is placed in the woman's fallopian tubes. p.336

Key People

Cowan, Carolyn & Philip: University of California psychologists who wrote the book, *When Partners Become Parents*.

Practice Test

1. About _____ of Americans surveyed say they never want children or are glad they don't have kids.
    A. 10%
    B. 4%
    C. 18%
    D. 7%

2. Cowan's Acceptance-of-Fate Partners, being told they were pregnant, would most likely react in the following way:
    A. "We really didn't want a baby, but we'll go ahead with it"
    B. "I want a baby, my partner doesn't, but I'll have it anyway"
    C. "What a pleasant surprise!"
    D. "A baby! Hallelujah!"

3. About _____ of Americans surveyed who have not had children say they want to someday.
    A. 84%
    B. 67%
    C. 93%
    D. 53%

4. Children as a percentage of the U.S. population are:
    A. increasing
    B. decreasing
    C. steady
    D. in a state of flux

5. Among women ages 15–29, fertility rates are highest among:
    A. high income women
    B. moderate income women
    C. low income women
    D. dual career women

6. For middle-income parents raising a child to the age of 22, in a two-child family, it will cost:
    A. $1 million
    B. $1.45 million
    C. $3.25 million
    D. $750,000

7. One researcher found that the average time for a sexually active couple using no contraception to conceive a child was:
    A. 6 months
    B. 10 months
    C. 2 months
    D. 2 weeks

8. The reaction of "We really didn't want a baby, but we'll go ahead with it" is most typical of:
    A. Planner Partners
    B. Acceptance-of –Fate Partners
    C. Ambivalent Partners
    D. Yes-No Partners

9. The cultural attitude that takes having children for granted is known as:
    A. pronatalist bias
    B. Down's syndrome
    C. child-free marriage
    D. anti-child free zone

10. "Only"children can be best described as:
    A. spoiled
    B. more self-confident
    C. lonely
    D. selfish

11. The text lists reasons that influence people to have children, they are all of the following EXCEPT:
    A. for religious reasons
    B. it will add to their happiness
    C. it will add another worker in the family unit
    D. to be accepted by their friends

12. In the U.S. today, most parents are opting to have:
    A. one child
    B. two children
    C. three children
    D. four or more children

13. Fertility rates vary for different ethnic and racial groups, with _____ having the highest rates.
    A. African-Americans
    B. Hispanics
    C. Whites
    D. Asian-Americans

14. In general, though not invariably, the more education and income a woman has the _____ the fertility rate.
   A.   higher
   B.   the more unpredictable
   C.   the less stable
   D.   lower

15. "Douching":
   A.   delays fertility in many women after childbirth
   B.   is rinsing the vagina with a chemical solution right after intercourse
   C.   is an antiviral, antibacterial spermicidal agent
   D.   is a contraceptive method proven to be highly successful

16. The avoidance of sexual intercourse during perceived fertile periods of a woman's menstrual cycle is known as:
   A.   sterilization
   B.   the barrier method
   C.   periodic abstinence
   D.   the hormonal method

17. "Coitus interruptus":
   A.   is a soft latex rubber dome over a metal spring or ring
   B.   consists of removing the penis from the vagina before ejaculation
   C.   is another name for the rhythm method of contraception
   D.   uses physical barriers between sperm and egg

18. Tubal ligation:
   A.   makes a pair of incisions in the scrotum and cuts the sperm-carrying tubes
   B.   blocks or cuts the fallopian tubes to prevent the egg entering the uterus
   C.   is the nonsurgical interruption of a person's reproductive capacity
   D.   allows for monthly hormone shots given in the arm, buttocks, or thigh

19. An abortion can happen spontaneously, owing to medical, hormonal, genetic, or other problems; this is called:
   A.   abortion ordinary
   B.   induced abortion
   C.   miscarriage
   D.   elective abortion

20. Almost half of the 6.3 million pregnancies that occur in the U.S. every year were not planned; of these _____ are terminated by induced abortion.
   A.   one-quarter
   B.   almost half
   C.   one-sixteenth
   D.   approximately two-thirds

21. After anesthesia, the cervical canal is expanded, the physician then uses a small, spoon-shaped tool to scrape the uterine wall of fetal tissue—this is known as:
    A. dilation and evacuation
    B. vacuum aspiration
    C. prostaglandins
    D. dilation and curettage

22. All of the following are causes of infertility in couples EXCEPT:
    A. not enough sex
    B. too much sex
    C. sex at the wrong time of the month
    D. failure to use Vaseline as a vaginal lubricant

23. "Endometriosis":
    A. is failure to ovulate
    B. creates an inhospitable environment for sperm
    C. involves cells of the uterus lining growing in the pelvic cavity
    D. refers to the failure to conceive after 1 year of sexual intercourse

24. The egg and sperm are taken from the parents and kept in a laboratory until the mother's uterus is hormonally ready; then the fertilized egg is implanted in the wall of the uterus—this is known as:
    A. gamate intrafallopian transfer
    B. in vitro fertilization
    C. zygote intrafallopian transfer
    D. artificial insemination

25. Adoptions in which the biological and adoptive parents exchange information such as photos and letters but don't otherwise communicate are known as:
    A. open
    B. semi-open
    C. public
    D. closed

Project Suggestions

Project 1
Abortion is an issue about which many Americans profoundly disagree. What is your point of view? What do you base your view on—politics? religion? friends? Can you see any common ground that people could agree upon?

Project 2
What do you think—do parents' sexual orientations affect the sexual identity development of their children? What are the positive and negative influences that same-sex couples bring to parenting?

Project 3
Many people become parents with little to no training. Should couples be required to take parenting classes? What type of information would be helpful for them to learn there? Would you be willing to attend a parenting class?

Answer Key

1. B (p.306)	6. B (p.307)	11. C (p.312)	16. C (p.316)	21. D (p.330)
2. C (p.307)	7. C (p.307)	12. B (p.312)	17. B (p.319)	22. D (p.333)
3. A (p.307)	8. C (p.307)	13. B (p.312)	18. B (p.323)	23. C (p.333)
4. B (p.307)	9. A (p.309)	14. D (p.312)	19. C (p.327)	24. B (p.335)
5. C (p.307)	10. B (p.310)	15. B (p.316)	20. B (p.328)	25. B (p.338)

Chapter 11   PARENTING:

Children, Families, & Generations

Learning Objectives

At the end of the chapter, you ought to be able to answer the following questions:
1.   Who are different people I might meet who could call themselves parents?
2.   What sorts of transitions might I have to make to adjust to parenthood?
3.   What kind of parent would I probably be, and how might I be a better parent?
4.   What should I be prepared for when I and my parents get older?

Chapter Summary

11.1   Parenthood: The Varieties of Experience
- If your family raised you with love and respect, you will probably bring this positive picture of parenthood to your own parenting.
- Teen parents often face a number of problems, with teenage mothers often ending up as single parents and poorer and less educated than other mothers. Divorced women with children often don't do as well as their ex-husbands financially and might suffer a marked decline in living standards.
- Changes in the U.S. economy often require that both parents work outside the home, which can lead to conflict over staying home with one's children or working outside the home.
- Families can be viewed along a continuum from being dysfunctional to functional. A dysfunctional family is one in which the parents demonstrate negative or destructive behavior toward each other or toward the children.
- Children are influenced by their parents, biology and heredity, the social environment, siblings and relatives, teachers, friends, and the media.

11.2   Becoming a Parent
- Pregnancy and childbirth involve both physical and psychological adjustments.
- After the baby is born, parents often undergo postpartum adjustment, a 3-month period of critical family and emotional adjustments, including bonding of the mother and child, postpartum blues, and postpartum depression.
- Adjusting to parenting requires that a couple devote their energies and finances to dealing with the various adjustments.

- The transition to parenthood can be more difficult than the transition required for other adult roles such as getting married or starting a new job.
- Transition to motherhood and fatherhood can be helped or hindered by one's family upbringing and socialization.

11.3   Parenting Approaches
- New parents' parenting style is heavily influenced by the type of parenting they received themselves.
- Three general approaches to parenting have been identified: authoritarian, permissive, and authoritative.
- Five parenting styles have been identified: martyr parenting style, pal parenting style, police officer parenting style, teacher-counselor parenting style, and athletic coach parenting style.
- Some child-rearing principles that have been found to help in effective parenting include (1) positive reinforcement, (2) instilling values and a sense of responsibility, (3) practicing good communication, and (4) avoiding physical punishment.

11.4   The Aging Family: When Parents & Children Get Older
- As parents enter middle age, they might find themselves members of the sandwich generation, taking care of both their children and their own aging parents.
- Since most elderly needy parents are not supported by the government, they are largely supported by family and friends.
- Grandparents gain self-esteem from playing such roles as historian, mentor, role model, storyteller, and nurturer.
- Five ways in which grandparents interact with the grandchildren have been described as the distant figure, the formal grandparent, the reservoir of family wisdom, the fun seeker, and the surrogate parent.
- Most people become grandparents in their forties and fifties, but blacks differ from whites in that they are apt to become grandparents at younger ages. Older adults without children have less chance of having a family support system.

Chapter Outline

- We first describe the status and rights of children and different kinds of people who make up the category *parents*; we then consider the role of a dysfunctional family background in parenting and show that other factors influence child development besides parents. We next consider both the mother's and the father's adjustment to pregnancy an childbirth and the transition to parenting. We then describe three parenting approaches and five parenting styles and consider ways to be an effective parent. Finally, we consider the aging family and grandparenting.

11.1 PARENTHOOD: THE VARIETIES OF EXPERIENCE

Major Question: Who are different people I might meet who could call themselves parents?

a.   The Status & Rights of Children
    i.   High Mortality Rate for Babies
        1.   In 2000, 6.9 of every 1,000 babies in the U.S. did not survive past their first year of life.
    ii.   Low Birth Weight
        1.   Infants weighing less than 3.5 pounds at birth are 40 times more likely to die within the first month of life.
    iii. Childhood Poverty
        1.   The child poverty rate for whites was 16%, blacks 30%, Hispanics 28%.
    iv.   Why Are So Many American Children Suffering?
        1.   Economics, poor health care system, two parents working, divorce and single motherhood, are all factors in children suffering.

b.   Young Parents: Teen Pregnancies
    i.   Difficulties for the Parent
        1.   Research shows that teenage girls who have babies end up poorer and less educated than other women.
    ii.   Difficulties for the Child
        1.   Children of teen parents have higher incidence of substance abuse, fighting, breaking the law, and failing in school.

c.   Single Parents: Unmarried & Divorced
    i.   Unmarried Parents
        1.   Increasing numbers of new mothers of all ages are unmarried.
    ii.   Divorced Parents
        1.   Married adults now divorce two-and-a-half times as often as adults did 20 years ago and four times as often as they did 50 years ago.

d.   Older Parents
    i.   Birth control and education and career opportunities have allowed women to delay childbearing until their later years.

e.   Minority Parents
    i.   African American Parents: financial security is not enough to protect parents or their children from incidents of racism
    ii.   Latino Parents: now the largest minority group, stressing authority of the father and respect for the parents
    iii. Asian American Parents: believe in educational success, and emphasize the authority of the family
    iv.   Native American Parents: stress a sense of family and tribal unity

f.   Nontraditional Parents: Single Fathers, Relatives, & Gays & Lesbians
    i.   Single Fathers: 2.2 million households in which single men were

raising children, a 62% increase since 1990
   ii.. Grandparents & Other Relatives: relatives increasingly are raising children when parents are incapable
   iii. Gays & Lesbians: in 2000 there were 60,000 male couples with children, and 96,000 female couple households with children
g. Working Parents
   i. In 1998, 78% of mothers with children ages 6–13 were working
   ii. Career-Parenting Conflict: a stay-at-home parent may find their role devalued by others
   iii. Parental & Maternal Leave: in 1993 Congress passed legislation allowing unpaid family leave
   iv. Child-Care Services: the average family pays about 10% of its family income for child care
   v. Making Time for Children: professional women who take time out to marry and have children are far more content than those who put their career above all
h. Your Own background: Functional or Dysfunctional Parents?
   i. A dysfunctional family is one in which the parents demonstrate negative or destructive behavior toward each other and/or toward their children.
i. A Sense of Perspective: Parents Aren't the Only Influences on Their Children
   i. Biology & Heredity: genetics and physiology are important influences on behavior, thinking, and personality
   ii. The Social Environment: environmental influences are socioeconomic class, race, ethnicity, religion, geography, and family size
   iii. Siblings & Relatives: brothers, sisters, aunts, uncles, cousins, and grandparents are all influences on children
   iv. Teachers & Friends: children are influenced by teachers and friends
   v. The Mass Media: in all its forms, mass media has a tremendous effect on children's values and behavior

11.2 BECOMING A PARENT

Major Question: What sorts of transitions might I have to make to adjust to parenthood?

a. Adjusting to Pregnancy & Childbirth
   i. Pregnancy: The Mother's Story
      1. Mothers often experience morning sickness, nausea and vomiting that happen frequently in the early morning
   ii. Pregnancy: The Father's Story
      1. Some men identify with the woman's pregnancy so much that they experience similar physical symptoms.
   iii. After the Baby Is Born: Postpartum Adjustment
      1. The postpartum period is a 3-month period following the

birth, during which critical family and emotional adjustments are made.

    b.   Adjusting to Parenting
        i.   Transition to Parenthood
            1.   Transitioning to parenthood is more difficult than other adult role transitions.
        ii.   Transition to Motherhood
            1.   Nearly all women find motherhood a truly life-changing event.
        iii.   Transition to Fatherhood
            1.   Becoming a father represents a "moral transformation" in that it shifts men's priorities and sense of responsibility.

11.3   PARENTING APPROACHES

Major Question: What kind of parent would I probably be, and how might I be a better parent?

    a.   Three Parenting Approaches
        i.   Authoritarian Child Rearing: "Do What's Expected Because I Said So!"
        ii.   Permissive Child Rearing: "Do What's Expected Because You Want to Do it"
        iii.   Authoritative Child Rearing: "You Know What's Expected: It's Up to You"
    b.   Five Parenting Styles
        i.   Martyr: "There's Nothing I Wouldn't Do for My Kids"
        ii.   Pal: "My Kids & I Are Buddies Because I Want Them to Like Me"
        iii.   Police Officer: "If My Kids Don't Obey Me, They Get Punished"
        iv.   Teacher-Counselor: "I Want to Positively Shape Every Part of My Children's Lives"
        v.   Athletic Coach: "I Want to Encourage My Children to Do Well within a Framework of Family Rules"
    c.   How to Be an Effective Parent
        i.   Positive Reinforcement: Predictability, Praise, & Love
        ii.   Instilling Values & a Sense of Responsibility
        iii.   Practicing Good Communication
        iv.   Avoiding Physical Punishment

11.4   THE AGING FAMILY: WHEN PARENTS & CHILDREN GET OLDER

Major Question: What should I be prepared for when I and my parents get older?

    a.   Parental Transitions
        i.   Role Reversal: Taking Care of Mom & Dad
            1.   Some parents find themselves sandwiched between taking care of their children and taking care of their own aging parents.

ii.   Relationships of Adult Children to Their Parents
1.   Most elderly people are not supported by the government.
2.   Both generations assume that children will assist parents.
3.   Emotional closeness of adult children to parents varies.
4.   Daughters are generally closer than sons to their parents.
b.   Grandparenthood
i.   Why Grandparents Like Being Grandparents
1.   Grandparents gain self-esteem by playing the roles of historian, mentor, role model, wizard, and nurturer.
ii.   How Grandparents Interact with Their Grandchildren
1.   The distant figure—"I don't see my grandchildren much."
2.   The formal grandparent—"I'm a grandparent, not a parent."
3.   The reservoir of family wisdom—"I know what's good for these kids."
4.   The fun seeker—"These little tykes are my pals."
5.   The surrogate parent—"I'm having to raise my kid's kids."
iii.   How Grandparents Interact with Their Grandchildren—3 Styles
1.   Remote—"I see my grandchildren only every 2–3 months."
2.   Companionate—"I see my grandchildren about once a week or more."
3.   Involved—"I see my grandchildren every day."
c.   Race, Ethnicity, & Grandparenting
i.   Asian Americans, Latinos, Native Americans, and African Americans are more apt to be involved in their grandchildren's Lives.
d.   The Childless or Child-Free Older Adult
i.   Older adults without children might have less chance of having a family support system.

Key Terms

Athletic coach parenting style: parents set rules for the house, helped by input from the family, teach the children the rules, and apply appropriate penalties for infractions. p.368
Authoritarian child rearing: parents are repressive, controlling, and often unreasonably strict. p.366
Authoritative child rearing: parents are, on the one hand, strict and controlling, yet, on the other hand, also warm and supportive. p.367
Bonding: close emotional attachment between parents and child. p.362
Continuous coverage system: in which parents must become fully responsible for a fragile infant—immediately, 24 hours every day. p.364
Corporal punishment: the use of physical force to cause a child to experience pain but not injury, with the intent of correcting or controlling the child's behavior. p.370
Dysfunctional family: one in which the parents demonstrate negative or destructive behavior toward each other and/or toward their children. p.357

Martyr parenting style: parents make great sacrifices for their children and exercise little to no authority over them. p.367

Morning sickness: nausea and vomiting that happen frequently in the early morning but also during other times of the day. p.361

Pal parenting style: also known as laissez-faire parenting—parents let children set their own goals, rules, and limits. p.367

Permissive child rearing: parents are warm and reasonable. p.366

Police officer parenting style: an authoritarian and repressive style in which parents insist that their children follow rules and punish them when they don't. p.368

Postpartum blues: a period of sadness and anxiety following giving birth. p.362

Postpartum depression: severe persistent symptoms of a major depression, which warrant the assistance of a health-care professional. p.363

Postpartum period: a 3-month period following the birth, during which critical family and emotional adjustments are made. p.362

Sandwich generation: parents sandwiched between taking care of their children and taking care of their own aging parents. p.371

Spanking: consists of hitting a child, usually on the buttocks, with an open hand without causing physical injury. p.370

Teacher-Counselor parenting style: parents are intensely focused on guiding their children's behavior. p.368

Key People

Baumrind, Diana: psychologist who identified three general approaches to child rearing; authoritarian, permissive, and authoritative.

Cowan, Phillip, & Carolyn: California psychologists that have identified changes that new parents might expect.

Furstenberg, Frank & Cherlin, Andrew: researchers who identified three styles of grandparenting: Remote, Companionate, and Involved.

LeMasters, E. E., & DeFrain, John: researchers who identified five parenting styles.

Neugarten, Bernice, & Weinstein, Karol: researchers who identified five types of interactive behavior between grandparents and grandchildren.

Rossi, Alice: sociologist who identified significant transitions of a couple becoming parents.

Practice Test

1. Almost ____ of high school students say they get along very well or even extremely well with their parents or guardians, a 2003 survey found.
   A. 75%
   B. 60%
   C. 43%
   D. 28%

2. The popular media expresses all the following ideas about having children EXCEPT:
   A. raising children will be fun
   B. it takes hard work and self-sacrifice to be an effective parent
   C. good parents raise good children
   D. just give kids enough love, and they'll turn out all right

3. If the family in which you were raised was a healthy _____ family, then you were raised with love and respect.
   A. rational
   B. dysfunctional
   C. functional
   D. cognitive

4. The United States has a child poverty rate of ____, the highest among 19 rich nations.
   A. 14.8%
   B. 23.7%
   C. 37.6%
   D. 43.2%

5. Although the teen pregnancy rate seems to be declining, about ____ of 1,000 girls ages 15–17 become pregnant each year.
   A. 7
   B. 13
   C. 27
   D. 32

6. Among parents who divorce, the mother winds up with custody of the children ____ of the time.
   A. 65%
   B. 90%
   C. 84%
   D. 98%

7. One study found that physical force, such as spanking, was inflicted by ___ of parents of children ages 3 and 4.
   A. 78%
   B. 84%
   C. 98%
   D. 94%

8. Research shows that teenage girls who have babies end up _____ than other women.
   A. more unhappy
   B. poorer
   C. more depressed
   D. less healthy

9. The probability of a first marriage ending in separation or divorce within the first five years is ____.
   A. 5%
   B. 50%
   C. 20%
   D. 30%

10. A family in which the parents demonstrate negative or destructive behavior toward each other and/or toward their children, is known as:
    A. toxic
    B. aberrant
    C. dysfunctional
    D. random

11. A survey of 1,000 parents by Common Sense Media found that an overwhelming majority believed that unsuitable TV, movies, video games, and contemporary music:
    A. have no lasting negative effect upon children
    B. lead to violent, antisocial behavior in children
    C. have minor negative effects but are soon diminished in children
    D. negatively affect some children but not others

12. The 3 months following the birth of a child in which critical family and emotional adjustments are made, is known as the:
    A. bonding season
    B. postpartum blues
    C. postpartum depression
    D. postpartum period

13. The famous child raising book, *Baby and Child Care*, was written by:
    A. Phillip Cowan
    B. Alice Rossi
    C. Benjamin Spock
    D. Diana Baumrind

14. Research shows that becoming a father represents a _____ in that it shifts men's priorities and sense of responsibility, so the responsibility for children found its focus in working to provide for them.
    A. moral transformation
    B. spiritual illumination
    C. change of heart
    D. change of mind

15. Parents who are on the one hand, strict and controlling, yet, on the other hand, also warm and supportive, are best described as:
    A. permissive
    B. authoritarian
    C. authoritative
    D. fickle

16. The parenting style expressed as "I want to positively shape every part of my children's lives" is:
    A. athletic coach
    B. teacher-counselor
    C. martyr
    D. pal

17. In terms of effective parenting, getting children to do what you want would most likely be accomplished by:
    A. commanding forcefully
    B. consistent positive reinforcement
    C. requesting politely
    D. yelling loudly

18. According to one study, ____ of parents use verbal and psychological aggression to control children ages 2–17
    A. 75%
    B. 90%
    C. 35%
    D. 55%

19. Is spanking ever appropriate?
    A. no, it always teaches violence
    B. yes, when done in love
    C. researchers disagree, there is no consensus
    D. it all depends on the culture

20. Many retired people today take their social security at age:
    A. 65
    B. 62
    C. 57
    D. 68

21. According to one study of 2,095 Americans over age 80, as many as _____ saw or spoke to their children two to seven times a week.
    A. 50%
    B. 98%
    C. 85%
    D. 65%

22. The expression, "I'm a grandparent, not a parent," best describes the type of grandparent interaction known as:
    A. the fun seeker
    B. the distant figure
    C. the formal grandparent
    D. the surrogate parent

23. The expression, "I see my grandchildren about once a week or more," best indicates the style of grandparenting known as:
    A. remote
    B. companionate
    C. involved
    D. meddling

24. In general, it seems clear that the role of grandparent is affected most by the relationship with:
    A. their spouse
    B. the adult child
    C. the grandchild
    D. the child's mother

25. In terms of women over 30 having babies, in 1998 the figure was _____.
    A. 12%
    B. 43%
    C. 23%
    D. 5%

Project Suggestions

Project 1
Of the three parenting approaches, (authoritarian, permissive, and authoritative) which one did your parents use? How do you think it affected you? Which one will you use if you choose to have children?

Project 2
How do you feel about corporal punishment and spanking? Were you spanked? If so, how did it affect you? Would spanking be acceptable under certain conditions? What would they be?

Project 3
Are children affected by their exposure to the mass media? Go to *www.commonsensemedia.org* and explore the data on the media's influence on children. Do you agree or disagree? Why?

Answer Key

1. A (p.344)	6. B (p.347)	11. B (p.360)	16. B (p.368)	21. C (p.373)
2. B (p.344)	7. D (p.347)	12. D (p.362)	17. B (p.368)	22. C (p.375)
3. C (p.346)	8. B (p.350)	13. C (p.364)	18. B (p.369)	23. B (p.376)
4. A (p.347)	9. C (p.351)	14. A (p.365)	19. C (p.370)	24. B (p.376)
5. C (p.347)	10. C (p.357)	15. C (p.367)	20. B (p.372)	25. C (p.347)

Chapter 12   WORK:

Economics, Jobs, & Balancing Family Demands

Learning Objectives

At the end of the chapter, you ought to be able to answer the following questions:
1.   What economic factors affect my family situation?
2.   Which arrangement describes my family/work situation, and how would I like it to be?
3.   Which work-life strategy would best work for me?

Chapter Summary

12.1   Work, Wealth, & Well-Being
- Money is relevant to marriage and intimate relationships through its power to increase security, power, love, and freedom.
- Before the industrialization of society, the family household was the major economic unit; work and family were almost the same things.
- As a result of the industrialization, workers were expected to work long hours to meet the demands of production.
- As a consequence of the Great Depression of the 1930s, a more rigid work ethic evolved. Lost in this process was the idea that people should work fewer hours and enjoy more leisure.
- In the 1990s, information technology also significantly affected the nature of work. Things like fax machines, home computers, email, pagers, and cell phones have made further inroads into leisure time.
- In many parts of the industrialized world, states offer noncash benefits to workers, yet in the U.S. most noncash benefits are offered by employers.
- Income is the amount of money a household receives from various sources during a given period of time. Wealth, also called net worth, is the monetary value of everything one owns, such as property, stocks, and insurance minus debts.
- Sociologists view society as comprising social classes based on income and wealth.
- Inflation, the decline in purchasing power, and a two-tier labor market have resulted in the lower half of society falling behind financially, and the gap between the net worth of white families and minority families has widened.

- The poverty line, established in 1959, is officially defined as the minimum level of income the U.S. government considers necessary for individual and family subsistence.
- The feminization of poverty denotes the likelihood that female heads of households will be poor, owing to job and wage discrimination, high divorce rates, and births to unmarried women.
- Some of the consequences of being poor include: greater exposure to environmental toxins; poor diets; higher rates of chronic disease, higher mortality rates; higher homicide, imprisonment, and mental-hospital admission rates; and loss or lack of insurance.
- Welfare or government aid for those who can't support themselves, such as the unemployed, the disabled, and the poor, is no longer popular.

12.2   Changing Family Work Patterns
- Economic and social forces shape the roles expected and performed by men and women in intimate relationships.
- In the past, most families adhered to stereotypical sex roles; the man as the provider and the woman as the homemaker.
- A newer family form has emerged where the man is the househusband.
- Changes in the economy have put extreme pressure on the purchasing power of families; now husband and wife may choose to work outside the home.
- Working mothers often fall into one of these categories: captives, conflicted, copers, or committed.

12.3   Balancing Work & Family Demands: Some Practical Strategies
- Family and career both involve the performance of various roles.
- Role conflict occurs when the expectations of two or more roles are incomplete.
- Role overload occurs when others' expectations exceeds one's ability to meet them.
- Role ambiguity involves unclear or unknown expectations of other people.
- People handle role disruptions in a variety of ways as they attempt to juggle work and family demands.
- Role compartmentalization involves separating one's various roles within the mind so that the worries associated with one role (such as work) don't disturb one's feelings and performance in another role (such as home).
- Positive self-talk consists of giving yourself positive messages so that you can view a situation in beneficial terms.
- Time-management and task-delegation skills are also beneficial in handling the various expectations and responsibilities of maintaining a household and a career.
- Many families are able to employ customized work arrangements.
- Many individuals have the option of taking time off to handle various family responsibilities.
- Scaling down one's career may also be an option for working couples who can afford to take a reduction in income.

- Although many people assume that it is bad for children to have two working parents—especially a working mother—studies show that advantages do exist.

Chapter Outline

12.1 WORK, WEALTH, & WELL-BEING
Major Question: What economic factors affect my family situation?
- We first discuss the history of work and its effect on family, as well as unequal distribution of income and economic factors affecting families today. We next consider various arrangements of work and family life. Finally, we consider different strategies for dealing with work-life balance.
  a. How Work Has Changed
      i. From Work & Family to Families in the Workforce
          1. Instead of working out of the home, many family members became part of the labor force as wage earners.
      ii. More Working Hours, Less Leisure
          1. As the result of industrialization, workers were expected to work long hours to meet production demands.
      iii. Noncash Benefits: Alternative Community Welfare
          1. Health, disability, retirement, sick leave, and unemployment benefits, are often fringe benefits offered by employers.
  b. The Unequal Distribution of Income & Wealth
      i. Which Economic Class Are You a Member Of?
          1. A six-class model includes: (1) capitalist class, 1%, (2) upper middle class, 15%, (3) lower middle class, 32%, (4) working class, 32%, (5) working poor, 16%, (6) underclass, 4%
      ii. The Rich Get Richer, the Poor Get Poorer, the Middle Class Loses Ground
          1. During the late 20th century, the top fifth of household income earners increased significantly—from 43.3% in 1976 to 50.2% in 2001.
  c. Economic Changes Affecting the Family Today
      i. Long-Term Inflation & the Decline in Purchasing Power
          1. Adjusted for inflation the dollar doesn't have the same amount of buying power, so that $13 today won't buy you as much as $3 did earlier.
      ii. The Two-Tier Labor Market: The Bottom Half Slips Behind
          1. The two-tier labor market is one in which people at the bottom lack the education and skills of those at the top.
      iii. Poverty
          1. In 2001, the poverty line was $18,104 for a four-person family; 33 million lived at that level.

d. What about the "Social Safety Net"?
    i. Welfare for those who can't support themselves is no longer popular.

12.2 CHANGING FAMILY WORK PATTERNS

Major Question: Which arrangement describes my family/work situation, and how would I like it to be?

a. Traditional Families: Good-Provider Husband, Homemaker Wife
    i. The Good-Provider Role: Traditional "Man's Work"
        1. The good-provider role emphasizes that the man is the principal or sole economic provider for the family.
    ii. The Homemaker Role: Traditional "Woman's Work"
        1. The homemaker role emphasizes that the woman should be principally responsible for housework, child raising, and maintaining family ties to parents and in-laws.
    iii. "Mr. Mom" as the Exception: Men as Full-Time Homemakers
        1. The househusband, or stay-at-home dad, is a man who is a full-time homemaker.

b. Co-Provider Families: Husbands & Wives as Economic Partners
    i. Working Women
        1. The percentage of women in the workforce has risen every decade throughout the 20th century.
    ii. Working Mothers
        1. There are four types of working mothers: (1) captives, (2) conflicted, (3) copers, and (4) committed.

c. Single Working Parents
    i. In the U.S., 9% of households are headed by a man or woman raising a child alone.

12.3 BALANCING WORK & FAMILY DEMANDS: SOME PRACTICAL STRATEGIES

Major Question: Which work-life strategy would best work for me?

a. When Major Role Disruptions Occur: Overload, Conflict, & Ambiguity
    i. Role Conflict: "Different People Want Me to Do Different Things!"
        1. Role conflict occurs when the expectations of two or more roles are incompatible.
    ii. Role Overload: "I Can't Do What They Expect of Me!"
        1. Role overload occurs when others' expectations exceeds one's ability to meet them.
    iii. Role Ambiguity: "I Don't Know What People Want Me to Do!"
        1. Role ambiguity occurs when you don't know what others expect of you.
    iv. How Some People Reduce Role Disruptions
        1. Married working women are apt to try to reduce role disruptions by trying to work part time .

b.   Strategy #1: Mentally Separate Work & Home Roles
     i.   Role compartmentalization—separating one's various roles within the mind so that the worries associated with work don't disturb one's feelings at home
c.   Strategy #2: Use Positive Self-Talk to Replace Negative Thoughts
     i.   Positive self-talk consists of giving yourself positive messages so that you can view a situation in beneficial terms.
d.   Strategy #3: Develop Good Time-Management & Task-Delegation Skills
     i.   Some working spouses are as effective at employing management skills for their households as they are for their jobs.
e.   Strategy #4: Employ Customized Work Arrangements
     i.   Parents Work Alternative Shifts
     ii.   One Parent Is Self-Employed
     iii.   One or Both Partners Use a Flexible Workplace Program
         1.   Alternative work schedules include: part-time work, flextime, compressed workweek, job sharing, and work-at-home schedules.
f.   Strategy #5: Take Other Forms of Time Off
     i.   Take Unpaid Time Off
     ii.   Take Personal Time Off
     iii.   Use Sick Days for Family Reasons
     iv.   Take Children to Work
g.   Strategy #6: Scale Down Your Career—at Least for a While
     i.   One study found that scaled-back workweeks slowed down careers but didn't stop them.
h.   A Final Word: The Effects on Children of Mothers Working Are Not Purely Negative

Key Terms

Compressed workweek: employees perform a full-time job in less than five days of standard 8- (or 9-) hour shifts, such as four days of 10 hours each. p.407

Co-provider marriages or dual-earner marriages: in which both married partners are employed outside the home. p.399

Family and Medical Leave Act (FMLA): requires U.S. companies that employ 50 or more workers to provide up to 12 weeks of unpaid leave a year to employees with a newborn or newly adopted child, serious personal illness, or a seriously ill family member. p.408

Feminization of poverty: denotes the likelihood that female heads of households will be poor, owing to job and wage discrimination, high divorce rates, and births to unmarried women. p.394

Flextime or flexible time: consists of flexible working hours or any schedule that gives one some choices in working hours. p.407

Good-provider role: emphasizes that the man is the principal or sole economic provider for the family. p.397

Homemaker role: emphasizes that the woman should be principally responsible for housework, child raising, and maintaining family ties to parents and in-laws. p.397

Househusband or stay-at-home dad: a man who is a full-time homemaker. p.398

Income: the amount of money a household receives from various sources during a given period of time. p.388

Job sharing: two co-workers divide one full-time job. p.407

Labor force: wage earners who hired out their labor to someone else. p.385

Leisure: time not taken up by work in which to engage in freely chosen satisfying activities. p.386

Median income: the income midpoint—half of a population earns more, and half earns less. p.388

Positive self-talk: consists of giving yourself positive messages so that you can view a situation in beneficial terms. p.404

Poverty line: the minimum level of income the U.S. government considers necessary for individual and family subsistence. p.393

Role ambiguity: when you don't know what others expect of you. p.403

Role compartmentalization: separating one's various roles within the mind so that the worries associated with work don't disturb one's feeling and performance at home. p.404

Role conflict: occurs when the expectations of two or more roles are incompatible. p.403

Role overload: occurs when others' expectations exceeds one's ability to meet them. p.403

Telecommuting: working at home while in telecommunication contact—by Internet, phone, and fax—with the office. p.407

Telecommuting: working at home while in telecommunication contact—by Internet, phone, and fax—with the office. p.387

Two-person single career: in which the husband works outside the home and the wife helps the husband's career by being responsible for domestic tasks and child rearing. p.397

Wealth or net worth: the monetary value of everything one actually owns—such as property, stocks, and insurance—minus debts. p.388

Welfare: aid to those in need. p.387

Key People

Moen, Phyllis: author of the book, *Women's Two Roles: A Contemporary Dilemma*, in which she suggests there are four types of working mothers.

Pearce, Diana: researcher who coined the phrase, "feminization of poverty."

Practice Test

1. In terms of money, love, and a couple's relationship:
    A. money and love have no direct relationship
    B. money has many psychological meanings that affect couple relationships
    C. money and love are inversely related
    D. money and love, it's like speaking of "apples and oranges" –very different

2. According to sociologist Marcia Millman, money is a primary source of _____ in relationships.
    A. expressing love
    B. happiness
    C. power
    D. conflict

3. Journalist Dick Leider asserts, "Life never lacks _____; it is innate—but it is up to each of us individually to discover or rediscover it."
    A. purpose
    B. love
    C. mystery
    D. wealth

4. According to one Gallup poll, _____ of the respondents consciously chose the job or career they were in:
    A. 22%
    B. 74%
    C. 8%
    D. 41%

5. In 1998, ____ of mothers with children ages 6–13 were in the work force.
    A. 4%
    B. 37%
    C. 78%
    D. 94%

6. As a result of the Industrial Revolution, work and families were divided, and instead of selling what they produced, men, women, and children sold their _____.
    A. property
    B. time
    C. energy
    D. intelligence

7.   In response to exploitation, labor unions were formed and the result of their efforts was that between 1830 and 1930, work hours were reduced by _____.
      A.   half
      B.   a third
      C.   a fourth
      D.   two-thirds

8.   The idea that to increase employment more people should become consumers came from President:
      A.   Abraham Lincoln
      B.   Teddy Roosevelt
      C.   Franklin Roosevelt
      D.   Jimmy Carter

9.   A great many people—_____, according to one survey—would prefer more vacation time to more pay.
      A.   97%
      B.   88%
      C.   48%
      D.   35%

10.   According to the six-class model of Gilbert and Kahl, if your income was $100,000 plus, you would be in the:
      A.   lower middle class
      B.   capitalist class
      C.   upper middle class
      D.   working class

11.   In 1970 the median price of a house in the San Francisco Bay area was $23,000, yet by 1999 the price was $372,000; this is an example of:
      A.   exflation   C.   purchasing power
      B.   inflation   D.   selling power

12.   If the minimum wage had just kept pace with inflation since 1968, when it was $1.60 an hour, the minimum wage would have been _____ an hour in 2003.
      A. $12.34
      B. $ 8.46
      C. $ 5.15
      D. $13.44

13.   In 2001, the poverty line was _____ for a four-person family.
      A. $12, 347
      B. $23,852
      C. $18,104
      D. $14,984

14. The likelihood that female heads of households will be poor, owing to job and wage discrimination, high divorce rates, and births to unmarried women, is:
    A. simply a matter of poor judgment
    B. known as the feminization of poverty
    C. the result of dropping out of school
    D. a reflection of the two-tier labor market

15. Traditional families that emphasize that the man is the principal provider for the family are best described as:
    A. two-person single career
    B. good-provider role
    C. homemaker role
    D. househusband

16. An invisible barrier preventing women and minorities from being promoted to top executive jobs is known as:
    A. job quota
    B. the glass ceiling
    C. WASP land
    D. token wall

17. In the Moen model of four types of working mothers, the expression "I'd rather be a homemaker, but I have to work" best describes:
    A. the committed
    B. the copers
    C. the conflicted
    D. the captives

18. In the Moen model of four types of working mothers, the "conflicted" would say:
    A. "I'd rather be a homemaker, but I have to work"
    B. "I'm committed to both my career and my family"
    C. "I'll work if the job lets me cope with my family demands"
    D. "If the job conflicts with my family, I'll quit"

19. In the U.S. ___ of households are headed by a man or a woman raising a child alone or without a spouse or partner living at home.
    A. 9%   C. 17%
    B. 13%   D. 22%

20. When the expectations of two or more roles are incompatible, then there is:
    A. role overload
    B. role ambiguity
    C. role conflict
    D. role confusion

21. Separating one's various roles within the mind so that the worries at work don't disturb the feelings at home, refers to:
    A. role compartmentalization
    B. positive self-talk
    C. developing good time management techniques
    D. employing customized work arrangements

22. Employees who perform a full-time job in less than five days of standard 8-hour shifts, are doing:
    A. flextime
    B. part-time work
    C. job sharing
    D. a compressed workweek

23. The law that requires companies to provide up to 12 weeks of unpaid leave a year to employees for family needs, is known as:
    A. Family Time Off Act
    B. Family and Medical Leave Act
    C. Required Unpaid Leave Act
    D. Employer Responsibility Act

24. One study of corporate professionals and managers found that scaled-back work weeks slowed down employees' careers but didn't stop them, in fact, about _____ were actually promoted after they started working less.
    A. 15%
    B. 25%
    C. 35%
    D. 45%

25. The positive effects on children of mothers working include all the following EXCEPT:
    A. more family money
    B. greater independence
    C. good female role models
    D. more quality time to teach values

Project Suggestions

Project 1
Of all the guidelines on choosing a good daycare on page 401, which point do you feel is most important? Why? What are your feelings about putting children in daycare centers?

Project 2
What kind of a money handler are you? Like to find out? Go to *www.moneyworkbook.com/finpers.htm* and take the 36-item test. Did the results surprise you? What did you learn?

Project 3
Will/does the career you have chosen conflict with your family life? How have you handled the conflict? What advice would you offer others in your life of work?

Answer Key

1. B (p.382)	6. B (p.385)	11. B (p.391)	16. B (p.399)	21. A (p.404)
2. C (p.383)	7. A (p.386)	12. B (p.391)	17. D (p.400)	22. D (p.407)
3. A (p.384)	8. C (p.386)	13. C (p.393)	18. D (p.400)	23. B (p.408)
4. D (p.384)	9. C (p.386)	14. B (p.394)	19. A (p.400)	24. C (p.409)
5. C (p.385)	10. C (p.389)	15. B (p.397)	20. C (p.403)	25. D (p.409)

Chapter 13 CRISES:

Managing Stress, Disaster, Violence, & Abuse

Learning Objectives

At the end of the chapter you ought to be able to answer the following questions:
1. What factors affect stress?
2. What are some major crisis events I might have to face?
3. What kinds of abuse are couples and families capable of?
4. What factors affect stress, and how can I handle it?

Chapter Summary

13.1   Stresses, Hassles, & Crises: Seeking Hardiness
- Stress is the reaction of our bodies to an unusual or substantial demand made on it. Stress has both physical and emotional components.
- Stresses are triggered by stressors, precipitating events that cause the stress.
- Hassles are simply frustrating irritants such as anxiety over wasting time and pressure to meet high standards at work or college.
- A crisis is an especially strong source of stress, a crucial change in the course of events that requires changes in people's normal patterns of behavior.
- One's psychological responses to stress is influenced by the number, kind, and magnitude of stressors.

13.2   Crises & Disasters
- Internal stressors are those events that begin inside the family. External stressors are those that begin outside the family.
- Stressors can be predictable and unpredictable.
- Unpredictable stressors include such crises as unemployment and underemployment, infidelity, alcohol and drug abuse, mental disorders, physical illness, and death.

13.3   Violence & Abuse: The Dark Side of Intimate Relationships
- Violence is the threat of or infliction of physical or emotional harm on another.
- Physical violence, or battering, is the infliction or threat of physical harm.
- Emotional violence, or emotional abuse, is verbal or psychological abuse that inflicts or threatens to inflict emotional distress.
- Violence can occur in dating, cohabitating, and marriage relationships.
- Dating violence can result from jealousy and sexual disagreements and/or be a consequence of the use of alcohol and drugs.
- Unwanted sex may range from people being forced to engage in sexual activities from kissing to sexual intercourse.
- Stalking is the repeated and malicious following or harassment of another person that may occur after that person tries to end a physically or emotionally abusive relationship.
- Marital violence is husbands attacking wives and wives attacking husbands.
- Patriarchal terrorism is violence by men who feel that they must control "their" women by any means necessary.
- The cycle of violence includes: (1) rising tension, (2) escalation and explosion, and (3) calmness, contrition, and kindness following the violent episode before the cycle begins again.
- Rape that happens within a marriage is referred to as marital rape and involves the use of force against one's spouse; it is illegal in every state.
- Individuals stay in abusive relationship because of fear of one's partner, of isolation, or of poverty or out of love, pity, duty, guilt, and hope that the relationship will improve.
- Family violence may be addressed through intervention, shelters, and safe houses.
- Women's safe houses are private homes that provide temporary housing for abused women.
- Treatment programs for abusers aim at changing the behavior of abusive men.
- Violence in intimate relationships is not confined to just adults; it extends to children as well.
- Risk factors for child abuse include a family history of physical punishment; unrealistic expectations for the child; alcohol or drug abuse; being raised in socially isolated, overcrowded homes; and economically stressed households located in low-income, unsafe neighborhoods.
- The effects of child abuse can last long into adulthood and may include physical and mental problems, emotional and developmental problems, and intimacy problems.
- Elder abuse consists of acts of aggression against the elderly.
- Elder neglect consists of acts of omission in the care and treatment of the elderly.

13.4   Coping Strategies: Successful Ways of Handling Stresses & Crises
- Stress in one's life can result from good and bad events
- As a result of distress, individuals may employ the use of defense mechanisms.
- Eight common defense mechanisms are repression, denial, rationalization, displacement, projection, reaction formation, regression, and sublimation.

- In handling stress, individuals adapt or cope with the stressors.
- To effectively cope with stress, you can reduce the stressors, manage your emotional response, develop a support system, take care of your body, and develop relaxation techniques.

Chapter Outline

- We first distinguish among stresses, hassles, and crises. We then consider some predictable crises of family life and then some unpredictable crises. Next, we describe various aspects of intimate and family violence and abuse. Finally, we discuss steps you can take to alleviate the stresses in your life.

13.1 STRESSES, HASSLES, & CRISES: SEEKING HARDINESS
Major Question: What factors affect stress?
- a. Stress & Stressors
  - i. Types of Stressors: Hassles versus Crises
    1. Hassles are simply frustrating irritants
    2. A crisis is an especially strong source of stress, a crucial change in the course of events that requires changes in people's normal patterns of behavior.
- b. Psychological Stress Reactions—Three Aspects:
  - i. Number, Kind, & Magnitude of Stressors in Your Life
  - ii. Your Emotional Predisposition & Self-Esteem
  - iii. Your Resilience
- c. Toward Becoming a Hardy Person
  - i. Hardiness is a combination of three personality traits—commitment, control, and challenge—that protect us from the potentially harmful effects of stressful situations and reduce our chances of developing illness.

13.2 CRISIS & DISASTERS
Major Question: What are some major crisis events I might have to face?
- a. Types of Stressor Events: Internal versus External
  - i. Internal stressors are those events that begin inside the family.
  - ii. External stressors are those that begin with someone or something outside the family.
- b. Some Predictable Stressors of the Family Life Cycle
  - i. The Beginning Phase: The Stresses of Newly Marrieds
  - ii. The Child-Rearing Phase: Stresses with Children
  - iii. The Middle-Age Phase: The Empty Nest—or Not
  - iv. The Aging Phase: Stresses of Health & Financial Worries
- c. Some Unpredictable Stressors
  - i. Unemployment & Underemployment
    1. Increases in depression, alcoholism, separation, divorce, infant mortality, suicide, violence against spouses, and

homicide are all associated with unemployment.
- ii. Infidelity: Sexual & Emotional Unfaithfulness
  1. Infidelity, or extramarital sex, adultery, having an affair, or "cheating," is marital unfaithfulness.
- iii. Drug & Alcohol Abuse
  1. Drug abuse, or substance abuse, is use of a drug in violation of legal restrictions or for other nonmedical reasons.
- iv. Mental Disorders
  1. Mental disorders are psychiatric illnesses or diseases manifested by breakdowns in the adaptation process and expressed primarily as abnormalities of thought, feeling, and behavior.
- v. Physical Disability & Illness
  1. Physical disorders may be acute, which are of short duration, or chronic, which are of long duration or are recurring.
- vi. Death
  1. The most severe family stressor is the death of a child, followed by the death of a spouse or parent.

13.3 VIOLENCE & ABUSE: THE DARK SIDE OF INTIMATE RELATIONSHIPS

Major Question: What kind of abuse are couples and families capable of?

- a. Violence & Abuse among Intimates: Some Definitions
  - i. Violence: the threat of or infliction of physical or emotional harm on another.
  - ii. Physical violence: is the infliction or threat of physical harm.
  - iii. Emotional violence: is verbal and psychological abuse that inflicts or threatens to inflict emotional distress.
- b. Violence in Dating & Live-Together Relationships
  - i. Causes of Dating Violence
    1. Daters become violent because of jealousy, when one person refuses to have sex, and/or because of excessive drinking or quarreling about drinking behavior.
  - ii. Unwanted Sex, Including Date Rape
    1. Rape is unwanted sexual penetration, perpetrated by force, threat of harm, or when the victim is intoxicated or unconscious.
  - iii. Different Experiences of Men & Women
    1. Men who were raised by physically abusive fathers might be apt to be verbally and/or physically abusive in dating relationships.
    2. There is no evidence that women raised by abusive fathers become themselves verbally or physically abusive.
  - iv. Violence in Cohabiting Relationships

1. Couples in live-together relationships are more apt to be physically violent than couples in dating relationships.
   v. Violence in Gay & Lesbian Relationships
      1. Research suggests that violence between gay and lesbian partners is the same as in straight relationships.
   vi. Stalking: The Abuse after Abusive Relationships End
      1. Stalking is the repeated and malicious following or harassment of another person.
c. Violence between Husband & Wife
   i. What Is the Incidence of Marital Violence?
      1. A study of 9 million married couples found that some violent episode occurred in one out of six marriages every year.
   ii. Two Kinds of Marital Violence: Patriarchal & Common Couple Violence
      1. Patriarchal terrorism is violence by men who feel that they must control "their" women by any means necessary.
      2. Common couple violence consists of violence between partners arising from everyday disagreements that have gone too far.
   iii. The Cycle of Violence: Three Phases
      1. Phase 1—rising tension
      2. Phase 2—escalation and explosion
      3. Phase 3—calmness, contrition, and kindness
   iv. Marital Rape
      1. Marital rape—forcible rape by one's spouse—is against the law in every state.
   v. Characteristics of Violent Families
      1. Domestic violence is found more frequently among young, low-income, blue-collar couples in which alcohol or drugs are abused.
   vi. Why Do People Stay in Violent Relationships?
      1. Fear—of partner, isolation, or poverty
      2. Love, pity, duty, guilt, hope
      3. Low self-esteem, childhood experience, learned helplessness
   vii. Escaping Family Violence
      1. The process of escape develops in five stages: (1) experiencing doubt, (2) turning point, (3) detachment and reevaluation, (4) shift in thinking, (5) breaking free.
   viii. Dealing with Family Violence
      1. Three important issues in addressing family violence include: (1) intervention, (2) shelters and safe houses, and (3) treatment programs for abusers.
d. Child Abuse & Neglect
   i. Risk Factors for Child Abuse

        1.   Risk factors include: history of physical punishment, unrealistic expectations for the child, drug or alcohol abuse, low-income, and unsafe neighborhoods.

    ii.   Effects of Child Abuse
        1.   Effects of child abuse include: physical and mental problems, emotional and developmental problems, and intimacy problems.

    iii.   Child Sexual Abuse
        1.   One study found that 27% of women and 16% of men had been sexually abused as children.

    iv.   Elder Abuse & Neglect
        1.   Elder abuse consists of acts of aggression against the elderly; elder neglect consists of acts of omission in the care and treatment of the elderly.

13.4 COPING STRATEGIES: SUCCESSFUL WAYS OF HANDLING STRESSES & CRISES

Major Question: What factors affect stress and how can I handle it?

a.   Good versus Bad Stressors
    i.   When the source of stress is a positive event, it is called a eustressor and its effect is called eustress
    ii.   When the source of stress is a negative event, it is called a distressor, and its effect is called distress

b.   Defense Mechanisms
    i.   Defense mechanisms are unconscious methods for denying, excusing, disguising, or changing the behaviors that cause anxiety and frustration.

c.   Adaptation versus Coping Strategies
    i.   Adaptation is not changing the stressor or the stress.
    ii.   Coping is changing the stressor or changing your reaction to it.

d.   Strategy for Living #1: Reduce the Stressors

e.   Strategy for Living #2: Manage Your Emotional Response
    i.   Be Realistic & Keep Control of Any Destructive Impulses
    ii.   Use Reframing to Feel & Act Positively
    iii.   Have Fun, Keep Your Sense of Humor, & Have Hope

f.   Strategy for Living #3: Develop a Support System

g.   Strategy for Living #4: Take Care of Your Body
    i.   Eat right, exercise right, sleep right, and avoid drugs

h.   Strategy for Living #5: Develop Relaxation Techniques

Key Terms

Acquaintance rape: nonconsensual sex between adults who know each other. p.435

Acute: of short duration. p.429

Adaptation: not changing the stressor or the stress. p.447

Alcoholism: a form of substance dependence, is defined as a chronic, progressive, and potentially fatal disease characterized by a growing compulsion to drink. p.427

Altruistic egoism: is the process of cooperation in which you help others satisfy their needs and they in turn help you satisfy yours. p.450

Anorexia nervosa: is self-starvation, resulting form a distorted body self-image that leads to the conviction that one is grossly overweight. p.429

Anxiety disorders: include four common mental disorders: generalized anxiety disorders, panic attacks, phobias, and obsessive-compulsive disorders. p.427

Bulimia: consists of episodes of binge eating alternating with purging. p.429

Child abuse: refers to acts of aggression by an adult against a child. p.442

Child neglect: is physical neglect, as in not providing enough food, clothing, health care, or security, or emotional neglect, as in not providing sufficient care, attention, and guidance. p.442

Chronic: of long duration or recurring. p.429

Common couple violence: consists of violence between partners arising from everyday disagreements that have gone too far. p.438

Coping strategies: are generally realistic and helpful ways of dealing with stress, pain, fear, and other problems caused by stressors. p.448

Coping: changing the stressor or changing your reaction to it. p.448

Crisis: an especially strong source of stress, a crucial change in the course of events that requires changes in people's normal patterns of behavior. p.417

Cybersex affair: a person has a secret online relationship with someone in an Internet chat room. p.424

Cycle of violence: consists of (1) rising tension, (2) escalation and explosion, and (3) calmness, contrition, and kindness following the violent episode. p.438

Date rape: nonconsensual sex between dating partners. p.435

Defense mechanisms: unconscious methods for denying, excusing, disguising, or changing the behaviors that cause anxiety and frustration. p.446

Denial: is the refusal to believe information that provokes anxiety. p.447

Discouraged workers: those who have given up looking for work and have simply dropped out of the labor force. p.423

Displacement: is redirecting one's feelings from the true target to a less threatening substitute. p.447

Distress: the effect of stress when it is a negative event. p.446

Distressor: when the source of stress is a negative event. p.446

Drug abuse or substance abuse: use of a drug in violation of legal restrictions or for other nonmedical reasons. p.426

Drugs: chemical substances other than those required for the maintenance of normal health, such as food. p.426

Eating disorders: consist of anorexia, or self-starvation, and bulimia, or binge-eating. p.428

Elder abuse: consists of acts of aggression against the elderly—physical assaults, emotional humiliation, verbal abuse, financial exploitation, isolation from friends. p.445

Elder neglect: consists of acts of omission in the care and treatment of the elderly. (p.445)

Emotional violence, or emotional abuse: is verbal and psychological abuse that inflict or threatens to inflict emotional distress. p.434

Eustress: the effect of stress when it is a positive event. p.446

Eustressor: when the source of stress is a positive event. p.446

External stressors: those events that begin with someone or something outside the family. p.420

Extrafamilial abuse: sexual child abuse by nonrelated individuals. p.444

Granny dumping: abandoning an elderly person at a hospital entrance with no identification. p.445

Hardiness: a combination of three personality traits—commitment, control, and challenge—that protect us from the potentially harmful effects of stressful situations and reduce our chances of developing illness. p.419

Hassles: simply frustrating irritants. p.416

Hedonistic affairs: acts of playfulness. p.424

Incest: sexual relations between persons who are related to each other. p.442

Internal stressors: those events that begin inside the family. p.420

Intimacy reduction affairs: involvements by a spouse who feels uncomfortable with too much closeness in his or her marriage. p.424

Intimate partner violence: physical and/or emotional abuse or one partner by another—male or female, married or unmarried, straight or gay, current or former. p.437

Intrafamilial: abuse: sexual child abuse by related individuals, including step-relatives. p.444

Learned helplessness: because of their battering experience, people perceive that they have no control over the major events affecting them. p.440

Marital rape: forcible rape by one's spouse. p.438

Marriage maintenance affairs: those that provide something missing from the marriage. p.424

Mental disorders: defined as psychiatric illness or diseases manifested by breakdowns in the adaptational process and expressed primarily as abnormalities of thought, feeling, and behavior, producing either distress or impairment of function. p.427

Miscarriage, or spontaneous abortion: the natural expulsion of a fetus from the uterus before birth. p.431

Mood disorders: mental disorders usually characterized by periods of depression, sometimes alternating with periods of elevated mood. p.428

Patriarchal terrorism: violence by men who feel that they must control "their" women by any means necessary. p.438

Physical violence, or battering: the infliction or threat of physical harm. (p.434)

Projection: the attributing of unacceptable impulses or characteristics to other people. p.447

Protection order: a court order that prohibits a person from threatening, harassing, or hurting a victim. p.441

Rape: is unwanted sexual penetration, perpetrated by force, threat of harm, or when the victim is intoxicated or unconscious. p.435

Rationalization: is the assertion that the reasons for illogical behavior are "rational" and "good." p.447

Reaction formation: occurs when people present themselves as feeling the opposite of what they really feel. p.447

Reactive affairs: are engaged in by partners, such as spouses in middle age, who are seeking reassurance about their youthfulness and sexuality. p.424

Reframing: you redefine the meaning of a situation as a way of changing your perspective on it. p.449

Repression: "motivated forgetting," the unconscious blocking of whatever is causing one stress. p.447

Resilience: various personal, family, or environmental factors that compensate for increased life stresses so that expected problems do not develop. p.419

Sandwich generation: couples who are sandwiched between taking care of their children and of their own aging parents. p.421

Sexual abuse: involves manipulated or coerced sexual behavior of a minor by an adult. p.442

Sexual assault: a legal term for rape. p.434

Spillover: the effect of participation in one of life's domains (such as work) on other domains (such as family). p.439

Stalking: is the repeated and malicious following or harassment of another person. p.436

Stillbirth: means the fetus is born dead. p.431

Stress: the reaction of our bodies to an unusual or substantial demand made on it. p.416

Stressor overload: unrelated but unrelenting small stressors can produce a breakdown in a person or family's morale. p.446

Stressors: precipitating events that causes the stress. p.416

Sublimation: socially constructive behavior that is formed to disguise unacceptable behavior. p.447

Substance dependence: differs from substance abuse in that the user becomes biologically dependent on the substance. p.426

Sudden infant death syndrome (SIDS), or "crib death": an event in which an apparently healthy infant under 1 year of age dies suddenly—and inexplicably—while sleeping. p.432

Underemployed workers: those who hold jobs below their level of qualification or are working part-time but want to work full-time. p.423

Unemployed workers: those seeking work who are new to the labor force or have been laid off, downsized, or fired. p.422

Violence: the threat of or infliction of physical or emotional harm on another. p.433

Vulnerability: the psychological or environmental difficulties that make children more at risk for developing later personality, behavioral, or social problems. p.419

Widow: a wife who outlives her husband. p.431

Widower: a husband who outlives his wife. p.431

Women's safe houses: whose existence is known only to residents and shelter workers, are private homes that provide temporary housing for abused women. p.442

Women's shelter, or victim shelter: provides not only food and accommodation but also other help such as money, food stamps, counseling, and legal, medical, and employment assistance. p.442

Key People

Johnson, Michael: sociologist who has identified two kinds of violence.
Masters, William, & Johnson, Virginia: famous human sexuality researchers.
Rosen, Karen, & Stith, Sandra: researchers who developed the five stages of escaping family violence.

Practice Test

1. The reaction of our bodies to an unusual or substantial demand made on it, is:
   A. pain
   B. stress
   C. distress
   D. exhaustion

2. Stresses are triggered by:
   A. stressors
   B. hassles
   C. crises
   D. frustrating irritants

3. In the U.S. the unemployment rate for blacks is _____ that for whites.
   A. three times
   B. one and a half times
   C. twice
   D. half

4. One study of a national sample of U.S. adults found that ____ of husbands said they had had sex with someone else sometime during their marriage.
   A. 15%
   B. 23%
   C. 32%
   D. 57%

5. In one study, ____ of 1,393 people ages 18–55 said that their partners, spouses, or children were or had been addicted to alcohol or drugs.
   A. 3%   C. 10%
   B. 25%   D. 36%

6. About _____ of people who survive a suicide attempt eventually do kill themselves.
   A. one-fourth
   B. one-half
   C. one-third
   D. two-thirds

7. One study of people who were dating, ages 30 and under, found that nearly _____ had either inflicted or suffered physical violence in their relationship within the preceding year.
   A. a third
   B. a half
   C. a fourth
   D. a fifth

8.   One national study found that _____ of women surveyed had been sexually abused as children.
A.   12%
B.   38%
C.   27%
D.   87%

9.   A crucial change in the course of events that requires changes in people's normal patterns of behavior, is known as:
A.   hassles
B.   crises
C.   stressors
D.   stress

10.   Various personal, family, or environmental factors that compensate for increased life stresses so that expected problems do not develop, is known as:
A.   vulnerability
B.   hardiness
C.   challenge strength
D.   resilience

11.   Stresses of health and financial worries would most be associated with what stage of the family life cycle:
A.   the child-rearing phase
B.   the middle-age phase
C.   the beginning phase
D.   the aging phase

12.   Those who hold jobs below their level of qualification or are working part-time but want to work full-time, are best described as:
A.   discouraged workers
B.   underemployed workers
C.   unemployed workers
D.   frustrated workers

13.   The phrase "Just for the fun and sensuality of it" best describes which Masters & Johnson's extramarital involvement type:
A.   intimacy reduction
B.   reactive
C.   hedonistic
D.   player

14. According to researcher Shirley P. Glass, _____ of all people who marry their affair partners end up divorcing them.
    A.   75%
    B.   96%
    C.   53%
    D.   33%

15. Alcohol, solvents, inhalants, would best be classified as:
    A.   hallucinogens
    B.   depressants
    C.   stimulants
    D.   excitants

16. About ____ of the U.S. population ages 12 and older are illegal drug users.
    A.   3%
    B.   8%
    C.   13%
    D.   17%

17. Panic attacks, phobias, and obsessive-compulsives would best be categorized:
    A.   mental disorders
    B.   mood disorders
    C.   emotional disorders
    D.   anxiety disorders

18. Self-starvation, resulting from a distorted body self-image that leads to the conviction that one is grossly overweight, is best known as:
    A.   bulimia
    B.   anorexia nervosa
    C.   an eating disorder
    D.   perfectionistic disorder

19. The term "battery" is also known as:
    A.   physical violence
    B.   emotional violence
    C.   emotional abuse
    D.   violence

20. Nonconsensual sex between adults who know each other is:
    A.   date rape
    B.   acquaintance rape
    C.   forced rape
    D.   familial rape

21. Violence by men who feel that they must control "their" women by any means necessary, is known as:
    A. common couple violence
    B. patriarchal violence
    C. intimate partner violence
    D. emotional violence

22. Phase 3 of the cycle of violence is:
    A. rising tension
    B. calmness, contrition, and kindness
    C. escalation and explosion
    D. actual pushing and hitting

23. Sexual relations between persons who are related to each other, is known as:
    A. child abuse
    B. sexual abuse
    C. incest
    D. sexual aggression

24. Acts of aggression against older people such as physical assaults, emotional humiliation, and verbal abuse, are known as:
    A. elder neglect
    B. elder abuse
    C. granny dumping
    D. senior violence

25. The attributing of unacceptable impulses or characteristics to other people, is known as:
    A. regression
    B. displacement
    C. rationalization
    D. projection

Project Suggestions

Project 1

Panel 13.1 on page 435 gives you ideas as to how to reduce the risk of date rape. As you read them, do other precautions come to your mind? What would they be? What would you say is the most important precaution?

Project 2

Do you know someone who has committed suicide? Have you ever thought about committing suicide? Go to *www.jedfoundation.org* and explore the ideas as to how to help reduce the suicide rate and improve mental health support for college students. What did you learn?

Project 3

People often wonder why some folks stay in violent relationships. Read again the reasons offered on page 439. Do they make sense to you? Can you think of other reasons someone would stay in a violent relationship? What would make you stay? Or go?

Answer Key

1. B (p.416)	6. C (p.417)	11. D (p.422)	16. B (p.427)	21. B (p.437)
2. A (p.416)	7. A (p.417)	12. B (p.423)	17. D (p.427)	22. B (p.438)
3. C (p.417)	8. C (p.417)	13. C (p.424)	18. B (p.429)	23. C (p.442)
4. B (p.417)	9. B (p.417)	14. A (p.425)	19. A (p.434)	24. B (p.445)
5. C (p.417)	10. D (p.419)	15. B (p.426)	20. B (p.435)	25. D (p.447)

Chapter 14   UNCOUPLING:

Separation & Divorce

Learning Objectives

At the end of the chapter, you ought to be able to answer the following questions:
1. What are the chances a marriage might end, and how might it happen?
2. What factors raise the risk that I might divorce, assuming that I were married?
3. What are the paths people take when they go through divorce?
4. If I were anticipating a divorce, what are some of the negative consequences I could envision?

Chapter Summary

14.1   Separation, Divorce, & Trends
- The American belief in the right to divorce seems connected to the search for happiness in intimacy and marriage. The term *uncoupling* describes the series of steps by which couples move toward ending their relationship.
- Besides death, there are four other ways in which a marriage can end: desertion, separation, annulment, and divorce.
- Before the 1970s, divorce was treated as an adversarial matter, with spouses attempting to prove each other legally at fault. Since then, divorce has evolved into a no-fault system.
- Community property—property acquired by a couple during their marriage—is supposed to be divided equally, reflecting the idea of equal contributions to the marriage.
- The ratio measure of divorce is the ratio within a given year of the number of marriages to the number of divorces. The crude divorce rate is the number of divorces in a given year per 1,000 population. The refined divorce rate reflects the number of divorces in a given year for every 1,000 married women over age 15.

14.2   Why People Divorce
- Divorce is more acceptable today than it used to be, in part because cultural values now mainly stress individual happiness over family togetherness.
- Lack of education is correlated with higher divorce rates. The younger the age at which a couple marries, the greater the chance that they will divorce, owing to lack of maturity and inability to handle marriage responsibilities.

174

- Personal factors that are associated with divorce include communication problems, infidelity, constant conflict, emotional abuse, falling out of love, unsatisfactory sex, insufficient income, physical abuse, falling in love with someone else, and boredom.

14.3   The Process of Divorce
- A psychological model of divorce consisting of six processes includes: (1) emotional divorce, (2) legal divorce, (3) economic divorce, (4) co-parental divorce, (5) community divorce, and (6) psychic divorce.
- The post-divorce mourning period consists of at least three stages, including denial, anger and depression, and acceptance and forgiveness.
- In divorce mediation, divorcing spouses make agreements with a third party about property division, spousal support, child custody, and child support. In collaborative divorce, a couple and their lawyers agree to dissolve the marriage without litigation and, if they fail, for the lawyers to drop out of the case before it goes to court.

14.4   The Effects of Divorce
- Divorce can have long-term consequences for an individual's emotional, psychological, and physical state.
- Some people experience positive effects of divorce—for example, increased self-esteem and feelings of competency, relief, and better relationships with children.
- Divorcing couples are affected financially by property settlements, spousal support, and child support.
- Divorce settlements are often intended to provide non-working spouses, especially displaced homemakers, with sufficient financial resources to live in their accustomed manner.
- Child support is the ongoing financial assistance for child-care expenses that the non-custodial parent gives the separated or divorced parent who has physical custody of the child.
- Two other systems of child support that are used outside the U.S. are: (1) a child's allowance, whereby the government provides a grant of child support to all families based on the number of children they have and irrespective of the parents' marital status or income level, and (2) guaranteed child support, whereby the government sends to the custodial parent the amount of child support payment that was awarded—then it's the government's task to collect this amount from the non-custodial parent.
- Child custody is the court-mandated decision as to which parent will be primarily responsible for the upbringing and welfare of the child or children.
- Divorce can have serious emotional effects on everyone involved, particularly children, and can result in parent alienation syndrome, divorce-related malicious mother syndrome, and child stealing.
- Short-term effects of divorce on children include guilt, anger, depression, anxiety, withdrawal, less social and school competence, and health problems such as eating disorders.

- Many children of divorce enter adulthood as worried, underachieving, self-deprecating, and sometimes angry women and men.

Chapter Outline

- The first section discusses different marital endings and trends in divorce. We next discuss the risk factors associated with divorce. We then describe the various processes of divorce, such as the emotional and the financial. Finally, we discuss the effects of divorce on the ex-spouses and on the children.

14.1 SEPARATION, DIVORCE, & TRENDS

Major Question: What are the chances that a marriage will end, and how might it happen?

    a.   The Continuing Search for Happiness: Are Our Expectations for Intimacy Too High?

        i.   High Hopes

            1.   Since the 1950s, people have increasingly emphasized individualistic values, stressing personal growth and self-fulfillment.

        ii.   Uncoupling: The Ending of Relationships

            1.   Uncoupling describes the series of stages by which couples—whether married or cohabiting, heterosexual or homosexual—move toward ending their relationship.

        iii.   What about "Divorce" among Gay & Non-married Couples?

            1.   Unmarried couples who live together—whether heterosexual or homosexual—must deal with the same kinds of issues, such as property distribution, alimony, child custody, and child support.

    b.   Marital Endings: Desertion, Separation, Annulment, & Divorce

        i.   Desertion: Abandonment & No Further Contact

            1.   Desertion means that one spouse simply abandons the marriage and family and has no subsequent contact.

        ii.   Separation: No Longer Living Together but Still Married

            1.   Informal separation: spouses settle financial, child-custody, child-support, and visitation arrangements informally between themselves; no legal papers are drawn up.

            2.   Formal separation: couples use a lawyer to draw up a legal agreement enabling them to live separately but specifying financial, child-custody, child support, and visitation arrangements between them.

        iii.   Annulment: Marriage Is Declared to Have Never Been Valid

            1.   Religious annulment: the Catholic church does not recognize divorce, but it does recognize annulment, which in essence declares that a marriage never existed.

            2.   Civil annulment: a state civil court declares that the

marriage was not valid, returns property to the respective partners, and allows both to remarry.

    iv.   Divorce: Legal Ending to a Valid Marriage

        1.   Since 1970 all states have adopted no-fault divorce, in which neither partner is found guilty or at fault; the marriage is declared unworkable and is legally dissolved for irreconcilable differences.

  c.   Trends in Divorce

    i.   What is the Most Useful Measure of Divorce?

        1.   Divorces are reported in several ways, such as, the ratio of marriages to divorces, the crude divorce rate, and the refined divorce rate.

    ii.   Today's Divorce Rates

        1.   Anywhere from 40% to 50% of new marriages will eventually end in divorce.

14.2 WHY PEOPLE DIVORCE

Major Question: What factors raise the risk that I might divorce, assuming that I were married?

  a.   Can a Happy Marriage Save Your Life?

    i.   One study found that the unhappily married were at higher risk for heart disease, high blood pressure, and cholesterol.

  b.   Societal & Demographic Factors Associated with Divorce

    i.   Family, Religious, & Legal Institutions: Have Changes Encouraged More Divorce?

        1.   At one time, family, religious, and legal institutions made divorce a difficult process, but as the U.S. changed from an agricultural to an industrial society, these institutions changed as well.

    ii.   Less Social Integration: Is Mobility Linked to Divorce?

        1.   Social integration is the degree of cohesion and strength of social bonds that people have with each other and their community.

    iii.   Individualistic Cultural Values: Is Individual Happiness Valued over Family Connections?

        1.   Since the 1950s, Americans have increasingly learned to put personal happiness and growth ahead of family connections and responsibilities.

    iv.   Education & Income: Do More Schooling & More Money Encourage Marital Stability?

        1.   In general, the lower a couple's educational level and income, the higher is the likelihood of divorce.

    v.   Age at Time of Marriage: Is Being Older Better?

        1.   People who marry as teenagers are more likely to divorce than are people who marry when in their twenties or older.

    vi.   Living Together: Are Cohabitors More Likely to Divorce?

1. Compared to married couples who did not cohabit, spouses who lived together before marriage have higher rates of marital separation and divorce.
vi. Pregnancy & Children: Does Having Children Before or After Marriage Affect Risk of Divorce?
1. Women who are pregnant or have a child before getting married are at higher risk for divorce than are women who conceive or bear children after getting married—at least for first marriages.
vii. Race & Ethnicity: Do National Origins & Culture Matter?
1. Race and ethnicity are often associated with education and income level that may be predictors of divorce.
viii. Divorced Parents: Does Being from a Split Family Encourage Divorce in Children's Marriages?
1. Parents' divorce may increase their children's probability of divorce within 5 years of marriage by 70%.
ix. Remarriage & Redivorce: Is Dissolution More Likely the Next Time Around?
1. For Americans who remarried during the 1980s, the divorce rate was found to be 25% higher than it was for people in first marriages.
c. Personal Factors Associated with Divorce
i. Communication Problems: "She/He Doesn't Know Me"
ii. Infidelity: "He/She Has Broken My Trust"
iii. Constant Conflict: "We Never Get Along"
iv. Emotional Abuse: "She/He Doesn't Treat Me Well"
v. Fall Out of Love: "My Perspective Changed"
vi. Unsatisfactory Sex: "The Thrill Is Gone"
vii. Insufficient Income: "There's Never Any Money"
viii. Physical Abuse: "He/She Beats Me Up!"
ix. Falling in Love with Someone Else: "This Is the Person I Should Have Married!"
x. Boredom: "It Was Just the Same Old Same Old"

14.3 THE PROCESS OF DIVORCE

Major Question: What are the paths people take when they go through divorce?
a. The Long Good-bye: Bohannan's Six Stations of Divorce
i. The Emotional Divorce: "I Don't Care for Him/Her Anymore: I'm No Longer Involved"
ii. The Legal Divorce: "I Wanted Out, but I Miss What We Once Had—& Why is the Legal System So Difficult?"
iii. The Economic Divorce: "I'm Afraid I Won't Have Enough to Live On, & I Dread Losing Things I've Become Attached To"
iv. The Co-parental Divorce: "He/She Can't Take Away My Children!"
v. The Community Divorce: "So Long, In-Laws; Good-bye,

Common Friends"
- vi. The Psychic Divorce: "Now, Finally, I Don't Care about Him/Her Any More; I'm My Own Person"
- b. Divorce Mediation & Collaborative Divorce
  - i. Divorce mediation is a process in which divorcing spouses make agreements with a third party about property division, spousal support, child custody, and child support.
  - ii. Collaborative divorce is when a couple and their lawyers sign a contract agreeing to dissolve the marriage without litigation—and if they fail, the lawyers pledge to drop out of the case before it goes to court.

14.4 THE EFFECTS OF DIVORCE

Major Question: If I were anticipating a divorce, what are some of the negative consequences I could envision?
- a. Emotional, Psychological, & Physical Effects
  - i. Divorce hangover: when one is unable to let go of the fact of their divorce, reorient themselves as single parents, or develop new friendships.
  - ii. Separation Distress: Depression, Anger, & Anxiety
    1. Separation distress: the psychological state following separation, which may feature feelings of depression, loss, and anxiety, as well as intense loneliness.
  - iii. Loneliness & Feelings of Being Stigmatized
  - iv. Stress
  - v. Health problems
  - vi. Positive Effects
    1. Perhaps surprisingly, many people say that being divorced yields positive effects, especially in the long run.
  - vii. Interaction with Ex-Spouse
- b. Financial Effects
  - i. Property Settlements: Are "Equal" & "Equitable" the Same?
    1. Equal-distribution: property that was acquired by either spouse during their marriage belong equally to the husband or wife.
    2. Equitable-distribution: the court determines a fair and reasonable distribution that may be more or less than 50% of any asset to either or the divorcing parties.
  - ii. Spousal Support & the "Alimony Myth": Are Better Arrangements Possible?
    1. Spousal support: the term that now consists of court-ordered financial support by a spouse or a former spouse to the other following separation or divorce.
  - iii. Child Support: How Well Does the System Work?
    1. Child support is the ongoing financial assistance for child-care expenses that the separated or divorced parent with

custody of the child receives from the non-custodial parent.

    c.   Effects of Child Custody Arrangements
        i.   Four Types of Child Custody
            1.   Child custody is the court-mandated decision as to which parent will be primarily responsible for the upbringing and welfare of the child.
        ii.   Issues about Child Custody: Hurt & Rage in Noncustodial Parents, Particularly Fathers
            1.   Father's separation—the loss to both parent and children.
            2.   Parent alienation syndrome—when children hate their parents.
            3.   Child stealing—kidnapping children from the other parent.
            4.   Supervised visitation—presence of a third party during visits.
    d.   The Effects of Divorce on Children
        i.   The Short-Term Consequences
            1.   Children in high-conflict families reported heightened emotional well-being and relief when removed from the scene of parental warfare.
        ii.   The Long-Term Consequences
            1.   Various studies report contrasting views.
    e.   The Good Divorce
        i.   A standard for a good divorce has not yet evolved.

Key Terms

Alimony myth: that most women profit from divorce by receiving high alimony payments. p.484

Alimony: court-ordered financial support by a spouse or a former spouse to the other following separation or divorce. p.484

Annulment: a pronouncement that declares that a couple never had a valid marriage, returning both partners to single status and allowing them to marry others. p.463

Birdnesting: the children stay in the family home and the parents alternate staying with them. p.488

Child custody: the court-mandated decision as to which parent will be primarily responsible for the upbringing and welfare of the child. p.464

Child stealing or child abduction: the act in which one parent kidnaps his or her children from the other parent. (p.490)

Child Support Enforcement Amendments: require states to deduct from fathers' paychecks and tax returns delinquent child-support payments. (p.486)

Child support: the ongoing financial assistance for child-care expenses that the separated or divorced parent with custody of the child receives from the noncustodial parent. p.486

Children's allowance: whereby the government provides a grant of child support to all families based on the number of children they have. p.487

Collaborative divorce: in which a couple and their lawyers sign a contract agreeing to dissolve the marriage without litigation—and if they fail, the lawyers pledge to drop out of the case before it goes to court. p.479

Community divorce: means that each partner reduces or leaves membership in a common community of relatives and friends. p.476

Community property: property acquired by the couple during their marriage. p.464

Co-parental divorce: involves decisions about child custody, child support, visitation rights, and the ongoing responsibilities of each parent. p.476

Crude divorce rate: the number of divorces in a given year per 1,000 population. p.464

Deadbeat dads: fathers who don't meet their court-ordered child-support responsibilities. p.486

Desertion: one spouse simply abandons the marriage and family and has no subsequent contact. p.461

Displaced homemakers: full-time housewives who lose their economic support owing to divorce or widowhood. p.484

Divorce hangover: they are unable to let go of the fact of their divorce, reorient themselves as single parents, or develop new friendships. p.481

Divorce mediation: a process in which divorcing spouses make agreements with a third party about property division, spousal support, child custody, and child support. p.479

Divorce: the legal dissolution of a valid marriage. p.463

Divorce-related malicious mother syndrome: a mother unjustifiably punishes her divorcing or divorced husband by attempting to alienate their mutual children from him, involving others (including lawyers) in malicious actions against him, and denying him visitation, telephone access, and participation in their school and after-school activities. p.490

Divorcism: the belief that divorce is harmful. p.467

Economic divorce: involves settlement of the property. p.476

Emotional divorce: involves loss of affection, trust, and respect for each other and replaces positive emotions with indifference or destructive emotions. p.475

Equal-distribution states: property that was acquired by either spouse during their marriage (except gifts from third parties) belong equally to the husband or wife. p.483

Equitable-distribution states: the court determines a fair and reasonable distribution that may be more than or less than 50% of any asset to either of the divorcing parties. p.483

Family Support Act: which authorizes judges to use their discretion when support agreements cannot be met and requires periodic reviews of award levels to keep up with the rate of inflation. p.487

Fathers' rights movement: which urges that divorced male parents have equal treatment with divorced female parents in matters of child custody, visitation, and support. p.488

Formal separation: a couple uses a lawyer to draw up a legal agreement enabling them to live separately but specifying financial, child-custody, child support, and visitation arrangements between them. p.462

Guaranteed child support: whereby the government sends to the custodial parent the amount of child-support payment that was awarded. p.487

Informal separation: spouses settle financial, child-custody, child-support, and visitation arrangements informally between themselves; no legal papers are drawn up. p.462

Joint custody: the children divide their time between both parents. p.488

Joint legal custody: children live with one parent, but both share decisions about their children's upbringing. p.488

Joint physical custody: children live with both parents, dividing their time on a more or less equal basis between the separate households. p.488

Legal divorce: the court-ordered termination of a marriage. p.475

Marriage sabbatical: a personal timeout from daily routines for creative, professional, or spiritual growth, for study, reflection, or renewal. p.462

No-fault divorce: neither partner is found guilty or at fault; the marriage is declared unworkable and is legally dissolved for irreconcilable differences. p.464

Parent alienation syndrome: a disturbance in which children are preoccupied with viewing one parent as all good and the other parent as all bad. The "bad" parent is hated and verbally marginalized, whereas the "good" parent is idealized and loved. p.489

Psychic divorce: which follows a period of mourning, means that you separate from his or her influence. p.477

Ratio measure of divorce: the ratio within a given year of the number of marriages to the number of divorces. p.464

Redivorce: divorces during second or subsequent marriages, with the median length of time for length of marriage declining in each instance. p.470

Refined divorce rate: the number of divorces in a given year for every 1,000 married women over age 15. p.465

Rehabilitative alimony: short-term financial payments to help a wife go to school and "rehabilitate" her vocational skills. p.485

Relatives of divorce: has been coined to describe kinship ties that were established during marriage but continue after divorce. p.477

Satiation: the term for what occurs when a stimulus no longer stimulates because of repeated exposure. p.473

Separation distress: has been given to the psychological state following separation, which may feature feelings of depression, loss, and anxiety, as well as intense loneliness. p.481

Separation: the state in which married partners decide to no longer live together. p.462

Six stations or processes of divorce: emotional, legal, economic, co-parental, community, and psychic. p.474

Social integration: the degree of cohesion and strength of social bonds that people have with each other and their community. p.467

Sole custody: children live with one parent, who is solely responsible for raising them, and the other parent has legally specified visitation rights. p.487

Split custody: the children are divided between the two parents. p.488

Spousal entitlement: a nonworking spouse receives a kind of severance pay for her or his "investment" in the marriage—for helping to advance the income earner's career during the marriage. p.485

Spousal support, or spousal maintenance: the terms that are now usually preferred to alimony, consists of court-ordered financial support by a spouse or a former spouse to the other following separation or divorce. p.484

Supervised visitation: in which a noncustodial parent is allowed to visit his or her child only with a third party present, such as a court employee or social worker. p.490

Third-party custody: in perhaps 1% of the cases, child custody is awarded to a grandparent, other relative, or some other adult instead of the parents. p.488

Uncoupling: describes the series of stages by which couples—whether married or cohabiting, heterosexual or homosexual—move toward ending their relationship. p.460

Virtual visitation: the use of such online tools as videoconferencing, webcams, and other wired or wireless technologies with which a noncustodial divorced parent can visit his or her child. p.474

Visitation schedules: the days and times on which the noncustodial parent is allowed to visit the children. p.464

Key People

Bohannan, Paul: proposed a psychological model consisting of six stations or divorce: emotional, legal, economic, co-parental, community, and psychic.

Hetherinton, Mavis: a developmental psychologist whose research indicates that divorce can be good for children.

Wallerstein, Judith: a clinical psychologist whose research indicate that divorce is bad for children.

Practice Test

1. Since the 1950s, people have increasingly emphasized _____ values.
    A. family
    B. individualistic
    C. fraternal
    D. self-centered

2. Blacks generally have _____ divorce rates than whites because they are disproportionately poor.
    A. higher
    B. lower
    C. modest
    D. unpredictable

3. One study found that in 47% of divorces, the leading cause of the breakup was _____.
    A. sexual dysfunction
    B. adultery
    C. incompatibility
    D. child rearing differences

4. Most people take _____ to work through the negative emotions of a divorce.
    A. 1 year
    B. 2–4 years
    C. 5–6 years
    D. 7–8 years

5. One study found that about 20% of fathers and 25% of mothers were still coping emotionally with their divorces _____ after the event.
    A. 5 years
    B. 8 years
    C. 10 years
    D. 15 years

6. One study found that 40% of divorcing wives lost _____ their family income, compared to 17% of men.
    A. half
    B. a third of
    C. three-fourths
    D. two-thirds

7. About _____ of men don't support their children at all after divorce—or even see them.
   A. 30%
   B. 80%
   C. 10%
   D. 50%

8. In terms of Vaughan's uncoupling stages, when one spouse eventually decides that continuing the relationship is no longer possible, it is called:
   A. further distancing
   B. turning elsewhere
   C. informing the other partner
   D. resolution

9. In a relationship, a personal timeout from daily routines for creative, professional, or spiritual growth, for study, reflection, or renewal, is called:
   A. desertion
   B. informal separation
   C. formal separation
   D. marriage sabbatical

10. If a person marries and is unable to have sexual intercourse, he or she or their spouse would probably seek
   A. a divorce   C. a formal separation
   B. a civil annulment D. an informal separation

11. The number of divorces in a given year for every 1,000 married women over age 15 is known as:
   A. the refined divorce rate
   B. the crude divorce rate
   C. the ratio measure of divorce
   D. the ratio of marriages to divorces

12. The median length of time for a marriage until divorce is about _____ years.
   A. 9
   B. 11
   C. 14
   D. 19

13. According to the text, in 1996 which country had the most divorces:
   A. Belgium
   B. United States
   C. Russian Federation
   D. Sweden

14. In general, the lower the couple's educational level and income, the _____ the likelihood of divorce.
    A. lower
    B. higher
    C. the more modest
    D. less likely

15. People who have started toward but fail to complete a particular degree or diploma, whatever its level, are _____ to divorce than those who secure a precise diploma or degree.
    A. less likely
    B. more likely
    C. not more likely
    D. absolutely likely

16. Compared to married couples who did not cohabit, spouses who lived together before marriage have _____ rates of marital separation and divorce.
    A. lower
    B. identical
    C. higher
    D. the least

17. Parents' divorce may increase their children's probability of divorce within 5 years of marriage by _____.
    A. 30%   C.   70%
    B. 50%   D.   90%

18. _____ problems were listed in one large study as the most frequent reason why Americans said they got divorced.
    A. Conflict
    B. Infidelity
    C. Communication
    D. Emotional abuse

19. Among the personal factors associated with divorce, the expression "The thrill is gone" best describes:
    A. boredom
    B. unsatisfactory sex
    C. falling out of love
    D. infidelity

20. In terms of the six stations of divorce, the expression "I don't care for him/her anymore, I'm no longer involved" best describes:
    A. the legal divorce
    B. the emotional divorce
    C. the sexual divorce
    D. the heart divorce

21. The divorce station which follows a period of mourning, and means that you separate from your former partner emotionally and are free from his or her influence, is:
    A. the psychic divorce
    B. the emotional divorce
    C. the mental divorce
    D. the heart divorce

22. The divorce mourning period consists of all of the following, EXCEPT:
    A. denial
    B. anger and depression
    C. acceptance and forgiveness
    D. rejection

23. When a divorced person is unable to let go of the fact of their divorce, reorient themselves as single parents, or develop new friendships, it is called:
    A. separation distress
    B. divorce hangover
    C. divorce stress
    D. physical effects distress

24. In terms of relationships among ex-spouses, those who have minimal contact, strive to avoid each other, and feel bitterness and anger when they do interact, are called:
    A. angry associates
    B. imperfect pals
    C. fiery foes
    D. non-cooperative colleagues

25. In terms of child custody, when some of the children are with one parent, and some with the other, this is known as:
    A. third-party custody
    B. split custody
    C. joint physical custody
    D. joint legal custody

Project Suggestions

Project 1
Did your parents divorce while you were growing up? (If not, find a peer whose parents did divorce) and make a list of the emotions and feeling you or your peer had at the time. Have you or your peer adequately processed these feelings? If not, would you or your peer consider talking to a counselor about them?

Project 2
Some people believe that cohabiting before marriage will make their marriage stronger. What did you learn from the text about cohabiting? Would you cohabit before marriage? Why? Why not?

Project 3
Check out the *www.divorcerecovery.net* website for helpful tips on the effects of ending a relationship and particularly how it affects children. What's the most important thing for divorcing parents to know and do with their children?

Answer Key

1. B (p.459)	6. A (p.459)	11. A (p.465)	16. C (p.469)	21. A (p.475)
2. A (p.459)	7. D (p.459)	12. B (p.465)	17. C (p.470)	22. D (p.478)
3. C (p.459)	8. D (p.460)	13. C (p.465)	18. C (p.471)	23. B (p.481)
4. B (p.459)	9. D (p.462)	14. B (p.468)	19. B (p.473)	24. C (p.482)
5. C (p.459)	10. B (p.463)	15. B (p.469)	20. B (p.475)	25. B (p.488)

Chapter 15 REMARRIAGE:

Reinvented, Renewed, & Blended Families

Learning Objectives

At the end of this chapter, you ought to be able to answer the following questions:
1. If I were a newly single adult, what should I be alert for in the dating scene?
2. How does a blended family differ from a nuclear family in characteristics and stages of development?
3. What are three perspectives of the stepmother, the stepfather, and the stepchild on the blended family?
4. What are the benefits of being in a stepfamily, and what are way to help ensure success?

Chapter Summary

15.1 Moving toward Remarriage
- During the last 50 years in the U.S., young adults have waited longer to get married for the first time.
- An urban tribe is an intricate community of young people who live and work together in various combinations, form regular rituals, and provide the support of an extended family.
- Many people in our society divorce before age 30, terminating what have been referred to as starter marriages.
- It takes some people longer than others to recover emotionally from separation and divorce. The transition phase lasts about 1 year; during this phase, one commonly experiences anxiety, loneliness, and depression.
- Some divorced people are in a hurry to remarry; reasons might be loneliness, need for financial or child-care help, and feeling that life is passing one by.
- Many individuals who start dating after the end of a relationship find that the situation is complicated by being the custodial parent of young children.
- Sex can also complicate new relationships after divorce or separation. Divorced men tend to enjoy sex more; their self-esteem is increased. Women do not find it quite as enjoyable; their sense of well-being is not linked to sexual activity.

15.2   Remarriage & Blended Children
- Although many divorced people think that the second marriage will be more successful than the first because of lessons learned from past experience, the second marriage is not necessarily affected by the first.
- In general, when both partners have been previously married, second and third marriages don't last as long as first marriages.
- Single remarriages—marriages in which only one of the partners was previously married—are no more apt to end in divorce than are first marriages.
- The postdivorce family is represented by single parents, binuclear families, and blended families.
- Blended families may be one of three basic types: (1) biological father—stepmother, (2) biological mother—stepfather, and (3) joint biological—stepfamily.
- Quasi-kin is the term used to describe the person a former spouse married, as well as any previous in-laws and new in-laws from remarriage.
- A genogram is a diagram that shows clearly all the people who genetically, emotionally, and legally constitute a particular family.
- Stepism is an attitude of prejudice and discrimination; it assumes that stepfamilies are inferior to biological families.
- There exist other more complicated family structures featuring adopted children, children from more than one former marriage, and siblings and half-siblings, some of whom live within the household and some of whom live somewhere else.
- Research has identified a number of characteristics of stepfamilies.
- Paralleling the stages one goes through in getting married or divorced, researchers have identified seven stages that are involved in the building of a blended family.

15.3   Inside the Blended Family
- One's experience of being in a blended family can vary according to who one is and the role one is expected to play.
- Stepmothers may find themselves in role conflicts involving the expectations that they be loving and accepting while also being disciplinarians.
- Stepfathers are apt to view themselves as less effective with their stepchildren.
- Stepchildren frequently have feelings of abandonment and being involved in conflicts between parents from the first marriage.
- The three major types of intrafamilial sexual abuse involve uncle and niece, stepfather and daughter, and stepbrother and stepsister.
- Sexual abuse may occur when four preconditions exist: (1) motivation, (2) inhibitions overcome, (3) obstacles overcome, (4) child's resistance overcome.
- Some suggestions for preventing abuse in stepfamilies are: arrange the living space appropriately, avoid being sexually provocative, curtail roughhousing and some intimate behavior with children over age 10, be affectionate but not passionate with your spouse in public, and don't turn to stepchildren for emotional support when you and your partner aren't getting along.

15.4 Strengthening Stepfamilies
- Stepfamilies have a number of potential benefits: families can be happier and calmer, with fewer crises and stresses, and might have fewer financial burdens; children can gain role models; parents might be more objective; children can gain more siblings and kin; and children can become more flexible.
- Influences specific to stepfamilies that help to ensure success are: harmonize finances, develop realistic expectations, let everyone mourn their losses, maintain the primacy of the relationship with one's new partner, treat children equally and give them their own space, don't rush being a stepparent, cooperate with the absent parent, develop one's own family rituals.

Chapter Outline

- The first section discusses the trend toward remarriage. The next discusses the characteristics and stages of development of blended families. We then describe the new family as viewed by the stepmother, the stepfather, and the stepchildren. Finally, we discuss some benefits of being in a stepfamily and ways to try to ensure its success.

15.1 MOVING TOWARD REMARRIAGE
Major Question: If I were a newly single adult, what should I be alert for in the dating scene?

a. Young Adulthood: "Urban Tribe" or "Starter Marriage"?
  i. Urban Tribes: Long-Term Friendship Groups That Help to Postpone Marriage
  ii. The Starter Marriage: Short-Lived First Unions
b. After the First Marriage: Returning to the Single Life & Dating Again
  i. Divorced People Who Date May Still Be in Emotional Recovery
  ii. Divorced People May Be in a Hurry to Remarry
  iii. Children Can Complicate the Dating Process
  iv. Sex Can Be a Whole New World
c. Middle-Aged Singles: Dating, Sex, & Lifestyles
  i. Dating
    1. The principal reason for dating was to have someone to talk to or do things with, and to simply have fun with.
  ii. Sex
    1. Twenty-one percent of men in their forties and fifties thought that sex on the first date is acceptable, but only 2% of women believed this.
d. Why Remarry?
  i. Midlife singles hate not having someone to do things with, and worry about being alone in the future.
  ii. Moving beyond Dating: Cohabitation or Remarriage?
    1. About a third of the men and women surveyed said they weren't sure about remarriage, a third said they would cohabit, and a third said they would remarry.

iii.   Reasons for Getting Married Again: Is It Time?
1.   The principal reason for remarriage was that "it was time," which probably expresses the need for intimacy.

15.2   REMARRIAGE & BLENDED FAMILIES

Major Question: How does a blended family differ in characteristics and stages of development?

a.   Remarriage: "This Time It Will Be Different"
i.   Happiness: Better the Second Time Around?
1.   Studies indicate few differences in marital satisfaction between couples in first marriages and those in later marriages.
ii.   Stability: How Long Lasting Are Later Marriages?
1.   As a general rule, second and third marriages don't last as long as first marriages.
b.   Blended Families & Kinship Networks
i.   Common Forms of Blended Families
1.   Biological father and stepmother
2.   Biological mother and stepfather
3.   Joint biological and stepfamily
ii.   New Kin, or "Quasi-Kin"
1.   Quasi-kin are any in-laws, both former ones from the previous marriage and added ones from remarriage.
iii.   Discovering Kin Relationships with a Genogram
1.   A genogram is a diagram that shows clearly all the people who genetically, emotionally, and legally constitute a particular family.
c.   Characteristics of Stepfamilies: From Sad Beginnings
i.   Most Stepfamily Members Have Suffered Some Sort of Loss
ii.   Blended Families Have a More Complex Structure
iii.   Family Boundaries Are Uncertain
iv.   Roles Are Ill-Defined, So There Might Be More Tension
v.   With Different Loyalties, Family Integration Comes Slowly
d.   Stages in Becoming a Blended Family
i.   The Turbulent Early Phase: Fantasy, Immersion, & Awareness
ii.   The Middle Phase: Mobilization & Action
iii.   Later Stages: Contact & Resolution

15.3   INSIDE THE BLENDED FAMILY

Major Question: What are three perspectives of the stepmother, stepfather, and stepchildren on the blended family?

a.   Being a Stepmother
i.   Expectations of Love & Acceptance by Stepchildren
ii.   Being a Disciplinarian
iii.   Problems with the Former Wife
b.   Being a Stepfather

      i.   Childless Man Marries Woman with Children
      ii.   Man with Children Marries Childless Woman
      iii.   Man with Children Marries Woman with Children

c.   Being a Stepchild
      i.   Feelings of Abandonment
      ii.   Conflicts
      iii.   Divided Loyalties
      iv.   Discipline
      v.   Stepsibling Rivalry

d.   The Special Problem of Sexual Boundaries
      i.   There are three categories of intrafamilial sexual abuse: (1) uncle and niece, (2) stepfather and stepdaughter, and (3) stepbrother and his stepsister.

15.4   STRENGTHENING STEPFAMILIES

Major Question: What are the benefits of being in a stepfamily, and what are ways to help ensure success?

a.   Five Potential Benefits of Stepfamilies
      i.   Families Are Happier
      ii.   Children Gain Role Models
      iii.   Parents Might Be More Objective
      iv.   Children Gain More Siblings & Kin
      v.   Children Become More Flexible

b.   Steps toward Becoming a Successful Stepfamily
      i.   Harmonize Your Finances
      ii.   Develop Realistic Expectations
      iii.   Let Everyone Mourn Their Losses
      iv.   Maintain the Primacy of the Relationship with Your New Partner
      v.   Treat Children the Same Way & Give Them Their Own Space
      vi.   Don't Rush Being a Stepparent
      vii.   Cooperate with the Absent Parent & Other Kin
      viii.   Develop Your Own Family Rituals
      ix.   Thinking of the Stepparent on Mother's Day or Father's Day

Key Terms

Binuclear family: a family in which former spouses and children live in two different households. p.512

Biological father-stepmother family: all children are biological children of the father and are stepchildren of the stepmother. p.512

Biological mother-stepfather family: all children in the family unit are biological children of the mother and are stepchildren of the stepfather. p.513

Blended family, or stepfamily: created when two people marry and one or both brings into the household a child or children from a previous marriage. p.512

Cultural script: set of social norms for guiding the various participants in their relations with each other. p.512

Double remarriages: marriages in which both partners were previously married. p.512

Family boundary: refers to rules about who is and is not considered a member of the family and the extent to which each member is allowed to participate. p.516

Genogram: a diagram that shows clearly all the people who genetically, emotionally, and legally constitute a particular family. p.514

Hidden agenda: expectations about how everyone should behave, but often these expectations are not communicated to everyone. p.520

Joint biological-stepfamily: (1) at least one child is the biological child of both parents, and (2) at least one child is the biological child of one parent and the stepchild of the other parent. p.513

Nuclear-family model monopoly: in which the first-marriage family is seen as the legitimate model for how families should be and all other forms are seen as deficient alternatives. p.510

Quasi-kin: the person a former spouse remarries or, more broadly, to describe any in-laws, both former ones from the previous marriage and added ones from remarriage. p.514

Serial marriage or serial monogamy: defined as participation in a sequence of marital partnerships, one at a time. p.502

Single remarriages: marriages in which only one of the partners was previously married. p.512

Starter marriage: a short-lived first marriage that ends in divorce, usually with no children and not much community property. p.504

Stepism: an attitude of prejudice and discrimination; it assumes that stepfamilies are inferior to biological families. p.510

Stepmother trap: the stepmother is expected to be unnaturally loving toward her stepchildren, yet she is viewed as being mean, abusive, and vain. p.521

Urban tribe: an intricate community of young people who live and work together in various combinations, form regular rituals, and provide the support of an extended family. p.503

Key People

Bohannan, Paul: an anthropologist who coined the term "Quasi-kin."

Paul, Pamela: editor of *American Demographics* magazine and author of *The Starter Marriage and the Future of Matrimony*.

Raphael, Phyllis: a sociologist who coined the term "the stepmother trap."

Practice Test

1. At least ___ of the ever-married population have been married three times or more.
    A. 1%
    B. 2%
    C. 4%
    D. 8%

2. Respondents in one study reported they spent an average of 17 months in courtship for their first marriage and spent _____ months in courtship for their second marriage.
    A. 9
    B. 17
    C. 23
    D. 27

3. A survey of 2,094 single women ages 40–69 found that _____ of unmarried American women who date were going out with younger men.
    A. a fourth
    B. a half
    C. a third
    D. two-thirds

4. Remarriages are _____ more likely to end in divorce than are first marriages.
    A. 8%
    B. 12%
    C. 16%
    D. 20%

5. About ____ of all U.S. children live in stepfamilies.
    A. 6%
    B. 9%
    C. 17%
    D. 23%

6. Only _____ states require stepparents to support their stepchildren, whereas all states require biological parents to support their children.
    A. 3
    B. 7
    C. 11
    D. 20

7. An intricate community of young people who live and work together in various combinations, form regular rituals, and provide the support of an extended family, is known as:
   A. a network family
   B. an urban tribe
   C. a rural group
   D. a city clan

8. A short-lived first marriage that ends in divorce, usually with no children and not much community property, is known as:
   A. a youthful social failure
   B. a starter marriage
   C. beginner's bad luck
   D. brief first union

9. During the _____ phase, which lasts 1–3 years, the divorced person's life and emotions have become more stable, with fewer pangs of loneliness, periods of depression, and moments of rage against the former spouse.
   A. transition
   B. recovery
   C. balancing
   D. settling

10. According to one survey, the principal reason for older singles to date was:
    A. to have someone to talk to
    B. to have sex
    C. to find a mate for marriage
    D. to expand their social circle

11. According to one survey, _____ of men in their forties and fifties believe that sex on the first date is acceptable.
    A. 12%
    B. 18%
    C. 21%
    D. 28%

12. According to one study the principal reason for divorced people to remarry given was "it was time" which probably expresses the need for _____.
    A. sex
    B. companionship
    C. intimacy
    D. commitment

13. An attitude of prejudice and discrimination that assumes that stepfamilies are inferior to biological families is known as:
    A. stepism
    B. stepfamily bias
    C. stepfamily prejudice
    D. stepfamilism

14. A number of studies have concluded that there are _____ in marital satisfaction between couples in first marriages and those in second or later marriages.
    A. major differences
    B. few differences
    C. significant differences
    D. no differences

15. In terms of the turbulent early phase of becoming a blended family the phrase "I think we're beginning to figure one another out now" is:
    A. stage 1 fantasy
    B. stage 2 Immersion
    C. stage 3 awareness
    D stage 4 understanding

16. In terms of becoming a blended family the phrase "No more Mr. Nice Guy with this family; I'm taking stand for myself" best describes stage _____.
    A. 1
    B. 2
    C. 3
    D. 4

17. The expectation for a stepmother to be unnaturally loving toward the stepchildren yet also viewed as being mean, abusive, and vain, is known as:
    A. the hidden stepmother
    B. the stepmother trap
    C. stepmotherism
    D. the stepmother anomaly

18. A remarried father whose children live apart from him and he spoils with treats is known as:
    A. spoiler dad
    B. Disneyland dad
    C. at-a-distance dad
    D. part-time pop

19. The most common perpetrators of intrafamilial sexual abuse are:
   A. uncles
   B. stepdads
   C. stepbrothers
   D. grandfathers

20. It is estimated that ___ of abused children in intrafamilial cases are females, and ___ are male.
   A. 75%, 25%
   B. 85%, 15%
   C. 95%, 5%
   D. 98%, 2%

21. All of the following are potential benefits of stepfamilies EXCEPT:
   A. families are happier
   B. children gain more siblings and kin
   C. children become more flexible
   D. parents might be more subjective

22. About ____ of adult children whose mothers had remarried were happy with the new union and half thought of their stepfathers as parents.
   A. 48%
   B. 24%
   C. 12%
   D. 64%

23. Stereotypes of stepmothers in literature picture stepmothers often as:
   A. indifferent
   B. uncaring
   C. wicked
   D. dangerous

24. In the U.S. today, one out of every ____ children is a stepchild.
   A. five
   B. four
   C. three
   D. two

25. A divorced, successful older man who has already raised children proposes marriage to a younger woman; pejoratively she is called:
   A. the eye candy wife
   B. the trophy wife
   C. the blue ribbon wife
   D. the "10" wife

Project Suggestions

Project 1
Go to *www.bonusfamilies.com* and explore the ideas offered as support for people combining families. What do you find most helpful? Did you observe anything you feel as unrealistic? Explain.

Project 2
Based on your understanding of the chapter what do feel are the biggest challenges facing blended families today? Can you think of anything you as an individual can do to help a blended family you know of?

Project 3
Interview three people who have been divorced and remarried. What did you learn about what people experience and feel as they go through divorce and remarriage? How did this experience affect your views on marriage, divorce, and remarriage?

Answer Key

1. B (p.502)	6. D (p.503)	11. C (p.507)	16. D (p.518)	21. D (p.528)
2. A (p.503)	7. B (p.503)	12. C (p.509)	17. B (p.521)	22. A (p.531)
3. C (p.503)	8. B (p.504)	13. A (p.510)	18. B (p.522)	23. C (p.500)
4. D (p.503)	9. B (p.505)	14. B (p.511)	19. A (p.526)	24. B (p.501)
5. C (p.503)	10. A (p.507)	15. C (p.518)	20. B (p.526)	25. B (p.501)